Primary Colours

Teacher's Book 5

Andrew Littlejohn   **Diana Hicks**

CAMBRIDGE UNIVERSITY PRESS

GW00691297

CAMBRIDGE UNIVERSITY PRESS

Cambridge, New York, Melbourne, Madrid, Cape Town, Singapore, São Paulo, Delhi

Cambridge University Press
The Edinburgh Building, Cambridge CB2 8RU, UK

www.cambridge.org
Information on this title: www.cambridge.org/9780521699914
© Cambridge University Press 2007

First published 2007

Printed in the United Kingdom at the University Press, Cambridge

A catalogue record for this publication is available from the British Library.

ISBN   978-0-521-69989-1   Pupil's Book
ISBN   978-0-521-69990-7   Activity Book
ISBN   978-0-521-69991-4   Teacher's Book
ISBN   978-0-521-69992-1   Class Audio CDs
ISBN   978-0-521-69993-8   Class Audio Cassettes

Contents

Map of Pupil's Book 5

Introduction

Primary Colours is a course in English for pupils of primary school age, who may be learning English in school alongside other school subjects or in a language institute. The course includes a *Starter* level, for complete beginners who have not yet learned to read or write. *Primary Colours 1* can be used after *Primary Colours Starter*, or with complete beginners who are familiar with print. This level, *Primary Colours 5*, is for pupils who have finished *Primary Colours 4* or who have completed approximately four years of English and who are now confident in all four skill areas in English: reading, writing, listening and speaking. The activities and content have been chosen to maintain pupils' fun in learning and to reflect the stage of their maturational development.

Each level of the course has these components:

- Pupil's Book
- Activity Book
- Teacher's Book
- Class cassettes / CDs
- Songs and / or Stories Cassette / CD for *Starter* and levels 1–3
- Vocabulary Cards for *Starter* and level 1

Pupil's Book

Primary Colours 5 Pupil's Book contains the following work for classroom use:

- a *Welcome!* unit with two sections.
- six main units, each with four sections. Sections A and C centre around a continuing story about three children who travel around the world on a magic carpet solving code puzzles set by Laya, who comes from another planet.
- Section B is called *Language time* and provides further practice of the grammar and vocabulary from the story in section A.
- Section D is called *Know it all!* In these sections the content of the unit is fleshed out with reading and listening activities which offer further information about the topic. They are followed by a related project activity.
- Units 2, 4 and 6 are followed by *Revision* sections.

Activity Book

The Activity Book contains:

- practice exercises for each unit, which the pupils can usually do at home if you prefer.
- six *Learning skills* sections featuring an English Control Panel as an on-going record of learning, and learning strategies for independent practice.
- three *Revision* sections, which include self-evaluation.

Teacher's Book

This Teacher's Book contains:

- a map of the course.
- teaching notes, which provide guidance on each exercise, extra ideas, answers and tapescripts.
- an *A–Z: teaching young learners* with many more ideas on teaching children.
- a *Games extra* section with additional games for practising new language.
- an optional photocopiable *Extra practice* section for each unit.
- photocopiable *Tests* for all units.
- a photocopiable *Assessment sheet*.
- photocopiable *Cut-outs*.
- *Word lists* for each unit.
- a *Flyers word list*.

Aims of the course

The main aims of *Primary Colours 5* are:

- to maintain the pupils' interest in and enjoyment of learning English.
- to broaden their lexical base.
- to develop grammatical competence.
- to increase confidence in communication.
- to improve reading, writing, listening and speaking skills.
- to develop awareness of effective learning strategies.
- to contribute to the pupils' education and understanding of the world around them.
- to encourage the transfer of thinking skills from first language to English.

Key features of *Primary Colours 5*

The key features of this level of *Primary Colours* take into account the importance of maintaining pupil involvement after four years of learning English. There may be widening differences of motivation and proficiency in your classes by the start of the pupils' fifth year of learning English.

This level offers a range of activities and content designed to include and support all pupils. *Primary Colours 5* expands the **topic-based approach** of the previous four levels to allow pupils to bring areas of personal interest to the classroom through their own knowledge of the different topics and project work.

Personalisation is a key factor in pupil motivation and throughout the book pupils are asked to keep their own English Control Panel. In this they record key words and sentences from each unit to help them remember what they have learned, as with the Time Travel Journal in *Primary Colours 4*.

Allowing pupils time, either at home or in class, to complete a record of learning provides an opportunity for them to choose aspects of the unit which are important for them, making the language and the content more memorable.

To help the pupils personalise other aspects of their learning, it is also important to encourage them to make decisions about what they will be doing and how they want to do it. This is particularly important in their project work.

Topic-based approach

As with other levels, *Primary Colours 5* is divided into six topic-based units with grammar and vocabulary carefully chosen to allow pupils to communicate their own ideas and to draw on information and experiences from outside the language classroom. This interdisciplinary approach to language learning leads to the use of richer and more varied language in the classroom and allows for important links to be made to other areas of the curriculum. It also develops the pupils' enquiry skills and offers learning strategies which will be invaluable at secondary level.

Learning styles

The topics and activities in *Primary Colours 5* recognise that every pupil is unique and that each pupil has different verbal, visual, aural, manipulative, musical and kinaesthetic skills. *Primary Colours 5* offers a wide range of creative exercises which are designed to bring out the best in every pupil and to maintain involvement. The learning skills sections in the Activity Book offer a wide range of strategies to help them develop their skills in speaking, listening, reading and writing. These activities can be introduced in the classroom and continued at home.

Making and doing

Many language learning activities require the pupils to 'do' something, for example, answer questions, fill in spaces or match two parts of a sentence. These activities provide the practice needed to help pupils absorb new vocabulary and grammar. In addition to these activities, many pupils respond well to an opportunity to 'make' an exercise as well as 'doing' one. The teaching notes indicate where it is appropriate to ask pupils to make their own puzzles, their own matching exercises, or to write their own comprehension and true / false questions for their friends to answer.

Primary Colours and Cambridge ESOL Young Learners English Tests

Cambridge English for Speakers of Other Languages (ESOL) has developed an assessment for pupils of primary school age who are learning English as a foreign language. They consist of three key levels of assessment: Starters, Movers and Flyers, with Starters being the first level.

If you are interested in putting forward your pupils for the Young Learners English (YLE) Tests, the most appropriate level is to prepare for Flyers after studying *Primary Colours 5*. The photocopiable Tests offer practice in some of the activity types used in the YLE Tests. In addition, the Flyers vocabulary syllabus is given on pages 134–137 with an indication of where words are covered in *Primary Colours 4* and 5.

Beyond *Primary Colours*

We trust that you and your pupils enjoy working with *Primary Colours* and that the course gives pupils the confidence to use English in a variety of situations. Above all, the aim is to give them motivation and strategies to continue learning English and other languages as they move higher through school.

Welcome!

A • The carpet

Topic

James, Alice and Gary help to clear out an attic in James' new house. They find an old carpet with a special screen and control panel. When they sit on the carpet, Laya appears and tells them that she is from Planet Zoon. She explains that the carpet can take them to her planet if they read six messages in code and find six special control cards but that they cannot return home if they fail to find the cards. James, Alice and Gary have ten seconds to decide if they want to go on this adventure.

Aims

- To revise language from *Primary Colours 4*.
- To introduce the characters: James, Alice, Gary and Laya.

Language

Revision
I have to tidy it first.
New language
attic, carpet, code, card, fail, message, press, real, serious, strange

What you need

- Cassette / CD and player.

Note: Please take some time to read the Introduction and the sections at the back of this Teacher's Book before you start using the teaching notes so that both you and your pupils can get the most out of the course.

Times: The times suggested are very approximate. Do not worry if your class takes more or less time for each activity.

Before you begin

The *Welcome!* sections revise some of the key structures from *Primary Colours 4*: present simple with adverbs of frequency, the infinitive of purpose, and *going to*. If you used *Primary Colours 4*, ask the pupils if they can remember the names of the characters, where they went and some of the adventures they had. You could also sing one of the songs from *Primary Colours 4* before continuing with the activity below.

If some of the pupils haven't used *Primary Colours 4*, you can go straight into the following activity.

Allow some time for the pupils to look through the book so that they can see what they will be doing.

Some ideas:

- Ask them to choose a picture which they particularly like or a story which looks particularly interesting.

- Divide the class into six groups and assign each group a main unit. Ask the pupils to tell the class four things about their unit, for example the title of the song in the A section, where the story takes place in either the A section or the C section, the title of the D section and the topic of the project in the D section.

Answer key and your notes

PUPIL'S BOOK pages 4 and 5

① Meet some people from *Primary Colours 5*. What can you say about each person? **6 minutes**

PURPOSE To introduce pupils to the characters and to stimulate the use of previously learnt vocabulary.

First, as a class, ask pupils to look at the picture of James. Encourage pupils to talk about him. They may say sentences such as *He is smiling. / He likes football.*

PAIRWORK Then ask pupils to work in pairs or threes and talk about the pictures of the other characters. Go round and help and then collect some of the sentences on the board.

Further practice: Activity Book Exercises 1 and 2.

2 Think. Say the names. 5 minutes

PURPOSE For pupils to find out more about the characters before reading the story and to practise the present simple and past simple.

Pupils work alone or in pairs to read and identify the characters.

3 What's new in your life? Tell the class. 7 minutes

PAIRWORK Give the pupils some time to think about what they can say about themselves and their family. They can first then work in pairs to tell each other their news. They then work in fours and tell the class. If you have a large class, it may be more useful to continue in groups.

Further practice: Activity Book Exercise 3.

4 Read and listen. What do the children have to decide? 15 minutes

PURPOSE To introduce pupils to the beginning of the story.

LISTENING TO THE STORY Allow time for pupils to look at the pictures and to read the text silently. Play the recording all the way through once and then again pausing between each frame. Ask the class to point to James, Gary, Laya and Alice.

Ask pupils to tell you the answer to the question *What do the children have to decide? (If they want to press the 'Start' button and go on the adventure.)*

Ask pupils whether they think it is a good idea to press the button.

New vocabulary: If pupils are not certain of a word, ask the class to make suggestions first before you provide the answer.

Further practice: Activity Book Exercise 4.

*Extra ideas: We have suggested extra ideas in each section. Some of these are whole class activities and some are designed for pupils who have finished a task before the others in order to give time for the slower pupils to 'catch up'. They are often suitable for inclusion in each pupil's **portfolio**. See A–Z: Portfolios on page 89.*

EXTRA IDEA Ask pupils to design their own magic carpet. They can draw it on paper or on a computer and then add different controls.

5 What can you see in James' attic? Look at the pictures for one minute. Close your book and write a list. 10 minutes

This activity may work better in a large class if you do it in groups. Allow one minute for each group to look at the pictures and then to close their books and write down as many words as they can.

Further practice: Activity Book Exercises 5 and 6.

6 Sing a song. *I've got a room in my house ...* 10 minutes

The words for all the songs are on Pupil's Book pages 62–63. The songs in *Primary Colours 5* occur twice on the recording: once with the words sung and once as a karaoke version.

Play the recording once or twice so the pupils familiarise themselves with the tune while they read the words. In previous levels, pupils have been encouraged to do some actions with the words, but at this age, many pupils may feel too old for TPR. Encourage pupils to join in with the recording. You could divide the class into two groups to sing alternate verses. Then swap verses so that everyone practises the different length lines as the song builds up.

The pupils can then work with the karaoke version, either with the same words as before or building up their own list of three items.

EXTRA IDEA The pupils could record their new version on tape or their MP3 players and put this in their **portfolio**. Pupils who play a musical instrument such as the piano or guitar could add an accompaniment.

See also **A–Z: Songs** on page 91.

ACTIVITY BOOK pages 4 and 5

Note: If the children use the Activity Book at home, it is important to look at the exercises with them in class first.

1a Find the words. The letters can go down, up and across. **10 minutes**

Pupils find the words in the puzzle.

1b Look at the other letters. Make a word. It's something that you can see on page 4 of your Pupil's Book **3 minutes**

Pupils make a word from the other letters.

2 Read the sentences. Four of them are about Sam, four are about Lucy and four are about Jack. Match them with the correct picture. **10 minutes**

Pupils read and match four sentences with each picture.

3 What's new in your life? Write sentences. **10 minutes**

Pupils write short sentences about what is new in their life.

4 Look at page 5 in your Pupil's Book. Answer the questions. **10 minutes**

Pupils read the story again and answer the questions.

5 Match the questions and the answers. **7 minutes**

Pupils match the questions with the answers.

6 Imagine you are in the attic. Are you going to press the *Start* button? Answer the questions. **10 minutes**

Pupils answer the questionnaire. Their answers are personal and the purpose of the questionnaire is to generate interest in the story.

Answers

P	L	R	D	B	I	K	R
W	A	E	A	M	W	E	E
E	Y	O	E	N	E	K	N
L	L	U	S	L	K	T	O
C	H	O	T	A	P	U	W

2 talk   3 bike   4 new   5 house
6 know ... well   7 read

Answer
computer

Answers
Sam: 2, 4, 7, 11
Lucy: 3, 6, 8, 10
Jack: 1, 5, 9, 12

Answers
2 Gary   3 James' parents   4 Alice and Gary
5 James   6 Alice   7 Laya
8 the children / Alice, James and Gary

Answers
2 = d   3 = a   4 = c   5 = b

B • Language time

Aims

- To practise the grammar and vocabulary from section A.
- To revise / introduce adverbs of frequency with the present simple.
- To revise / introduce *going to*.

Language

Revision
Adverbs of frequency with the present simple
going to

New language
made of ... cardboard, cloth, glass, metal, paper, plastic, rubber, wood
heavy, light, rectangular, round, square

What you need

- Cassette / CD and player.
- Copies of Cut-outs 1 and 2 (pages 127 and 128) for the Activity Book English Control Panel.

English Control Panel: *At the end of this B section in the Activity Book, we suggest that the pupils make an English Control Panel, which they will use throughout the course. The purpose of this is for the pupils to make a record of their learning in which they write some important sentences showing the new words and new grammar from each unit. They can use this to help them revise, and they can also look back at it when they reflect on their learning in the evaluation section in each Revision Unit (see page 28). You can check that each pupil has included the key structures but also allow them the freedom to add their own words and sentences so that they feel that their English Control Panel is unique and personal. You may want to leave some time for the pupils to make their booklet in class, so that you can check that everyone has done it.*

If anyone in the class didn't use Primary Colours 4 *(or if the class didn't make a Time Travel Journal), you can also take the opportunity to explain that this will help them understand the new vocabulary and grammar from each unit. You may also like to make an English Control Panel first so that the pupils can see what it looks like. See* **A–Z: English Control Panel** *on page 82.*

PUPIL'S BOOK pages 6 and 7

1a Read about James and Alice. What are their answers to the questions? Write 'always', 'usually', 'sometimes' or 'never'. **12 minutes**

PURPOSE To practise adverbs of frequency.

Allow time for the pupils to read the text and to complete the questionnaire.

PAIRWORK They can then ask and answer the questions in pairs – one answering as James and one answering as Alice. If you prefer, encourage them to use full sentences: *Yes, I (often) ... or No, I (never) ...*

1b Work with a friend. Ask and answer. **8 minutes**

PURPOSE To practise speaking with adverbs of frequency.

PAIRWORK Pupils work in pairs and ask and answer the questions.

Further practice: Activity Book Exercises 3 and 4.

Answer key, tapescript and your notes

Answers
James: 2 always 3 never 4 sometimes
5 never 6 usually
Alice: 1 usually 2 never 3 always 4 never
5 always 6 never

Answers

Amy's dad is going to put up some shelves. He's going to put the TV on the shelves. = e, f

Amy's auntie is going to give them a sofa. = d

Amy's brother is going to make some curtains. = a

Amy is going to clean the floor and the walls. = b

2 Listen. Amy is talking to Max about her family's living room. Match the people and the things. What are they going to do?

8 minutes

PURPOSE To practise listening intensively and to practise *going to*.

Allow time for pupils to look at the pictures first. Ask them to say what they can see. Then play the recording. Pupils match the people with the pictures, either by drawing lines in their books or by writing the correct names and letters in their exercise books.

Go through as a class afterwards eliciting sentences with *going to* as in the model.

Tapescript

Amy: Hi, Max. Come in. Look at this!

Max: What! What's happening here?

Amy: We're going to change the living room. My mum's going to paint the walls. Then my dad's going to put up some new shelves. He's going to put the TV on the shelves. You can see the wood there.

Max: Oh yes, I see.

Amy: Then my mum and dad are going to get a new sofa.

Max: Wow! That's a lot of money.

Amy: No, not really. It's not really new. My auntie is going to give us her old one!

Max: OK. What about the curtains? You haven't got any curtains.

Amy: My brother is going to make some curtains. That's what he **says**!

Max: Well, that's a big job.

Amy: Yes, I think so, too.

Max: Amy, what are **you** going to do?

Amy: Well ... I'm going to watch them and then I'm going to sit on the sofa and watch TV!

Max: Ha, ha! Amy, you're lazy!

Amy: Ha ha! No, I'm going to clean the floor and the walls before my mum paints them. Look, those are **my** things there. Do you want to help?

Max: Er, erm. What time is it? Oh no, I've got to go!

Further practice: Activity Book Exercise 1.

3a Work with a friend. Look at the picture of James' attic. Take it in turns to describe things for your friend to find.

8 minutes

PURPOSE To practise speaking and to practise shape, colour and materials vocabulary.

PAIRWORK Pupils work in pairs and take it in turns to choose an item in the attic. They describe the item using words from the box for their partner to guess what it is.

3b Match the descriptions with things in James' attic.

5 minutes

Pupils work individually and find things which match the descriptions.

Answers

1 a sofa   2 a door   3 a fridge   4 a book

3c Write more descriptions for your friend to guess.

10–15 minutes

PURPOSE To practise writing and to practise shape, colour and materials vocabulary.

Pupils choose other items and write similar descriptions.

PAIRWORK They exchange their descriptions with a partner and find the items in the picture.

Further practice: Activity Book Exercise 2.

ACTIVITY BOOK pages 6 and 7

1 Fred is going on holiday next week. What is he going to do? Write sentences. | 20 minutes

Pupils write what Fred is going to do on his holiday.

2 Look at James' attic. Find the things and number the clues. | 10 minutes

Pupils read the sentences and number the boxes.

EXTRA IDEA Pupils can choose other items and write similar sentences like this for their partner to guess the words.

Learning skills: A new start

3 Answer the questions. | 10 minutes

Pupils complete the questionnaire and work out their score. They read what this shows them about their learning habits.

4 Choose four questions from Exercise 3 and give a reason for your answer. | 10–15 minutes

Pupils write sentences about their learning habits as in the model, using adverbs of frequency.

Make your English Control Panel

Note: *See the note on making an English Control Panel (page 5). If you made a model, show this to the pupils before they begin. Make sure they have all the materials they need, including Cut-outs 1 and 2 (pages 127 and 128).*

Each pupil needs four pieces of paper (preferably A4 size) and copies of Cut-outs 1 and 2. They can share scissors, glue and a stapler in groups.

Pupils fold the four pieces of paper in half and staple them together. They number the pages 1–16 and then stick the cut-outs on pages 1 and 16.

They prepare the booklet for use at the end of each unit by writing the following headings first at the top of pages 2 and 3, and then throughout the booklet on pages 4–13:

Place: Important words to remember
and
Important sentences to remember

They write the title *Extra ideas* at the top of pages 14–15.

Explain that they will complete their English Control Panel at the end of each unit in the Activity Book and that this will help them understand the new vocabulary and grammar from each unit. Point out that they can also use it to help them revise. Ask the pupils to keep it safely and then, at the end of the year, it can be included in their **portfolio**.

See **A–Z: English Control Panel** on page 82.

Suggested answers

2 He's going to go to the beach.
3 He's going to eat / have lunch / dinner in a / the restaurant.
4 He's going to take (lots of) photos.
5 He's going to see the sea from his room.
6 He's going to watch TV.
7 He's going to go shopping.
8 He's going to swim / go swimming in the (swimming) pool.

Answers

12 a lamp   1 a fish tank / an aquarium
8 a table   10 a cap / hat   7 an umbrella
5 a book   6 a sofa   2 a coat   11 a bike
9 a box   3 a window

1A • Danger!

Topic

Gary presses the button on the carpet control panel without waiting for the others. Laya appears and shows them a message in code. Gary guesses the place and touches the map on the screen. The carpet flies out of the window and they eventually land in the Grand Canyon. Alice sees the control card in a hole and jumps in to get it, but three rattlesnakes appear.

Aims

- To revise *must / mustn't*.
- To revise the infinitive of purpose.

Language

Revision
We must decide now!
Why did Gary press the *Start* button? To see the first message.
New language
above, appear, below, button, decide, deep, desert, huge, immediately, rattlesnake, screen, somewhere, suddenly, together

What you need

- Cassette / CD and player.

The story: Continuing from the introductory episode, a continuous story runs through the book with episodes in sections A and C of each unit. The story centres around three characters who fly on a magic carpet which has a special control panel and screen. The children have to solve six coded messages, identifying the next place that they will visit, and then find a control card in each place. As Laya explained in the introductory episode, the children cannot return home until they have found all six cards.

Each place they visit is a world heritage site, which allows for the development of cross-curricular themes in each unit (see page vii). You can find out about world heritage sites on www.worldheritagesite.org.

*New language: There are new words in each episode of the story. You may prefer to extract these words from the text and pre-teach them through mime or translation before the pupils read or hear them in the story. However, pupils of this age are developing a greater ability to work out the meaning from the context together with the support of the pictures. As it is a continuous story, the pupils will be keen to know what happens in the next episode so it may be more productive to check their understanding of new vocabulary **after** they have read and listened to the story rather than before. Similarly, new structures are presented through the story, where the context supports the meaning, and structures from previous levels are also recycled. Pupils have further exposure to the new or recycled language in the follow-up comprehension exercises and more specifically in Section B: Language time.*

Before you begin

Sing the song from the *Welcome!* unit, section A.

Ask pupils what they remember of the story and the characters in the *Welcome!* unit.

Answer key and your notes

PUPIL'S BOOK pages 8 and 9

1 🔲 Read and listen. Why mustn't Alice move? **20 minutes**

PURPOSE To find out more about the carpet and the code and to practise listening, speaking and reading.

LISTENING TO THE STORY Allow time for the pupils to look at the pictures. Ask them what they can see and what they know about the Grand Canyon. Ask them to try and read the story before playing the recording. This will help with their listening comprehension.

Play the recording and ask pupils to find the answer to the question *Why mustn't Alice move? (Snakes are dangerous and if she moves, they can bite her.)*

Ask pupils to compare their ideas about how James and Gary can help her.

Further practice: Activity Book Exercise 1.

2 Read the story again. Say 'True', 'False' or 'We don't know'. **15 minutes**

PURPOSE To help pupils look more closely at the story.

Pupils can work alone or in pairs for this exercise.

Further practice: Activity Book Exercise 2.

Answers
2 False 3 True 4 False 5 We don't know
6 True 7 We don't know
8 We don't know

3 Match the questions and the answers. Complete the missing answers. **8 minutes**

PURPOSE To practise the infinitive of purpose.

Pupils match the questions and answers, complete the last two answers and then compare with a partner.

Further practice: Activity Book Exercises 3 and 4.

Answers
2 = a 3 = d To tell her about the snakes.
4 = e To get the first card. 5 = b

4 What must or mustn't you do if you see these animals? Tell the class. **12 minutes**

PURPOSE To practise the zero conditional and *must* / *mustn't*.

Allow time for pupils to look at the pictures and to read the phrases in the box. Check that everyone remembers *must* / *mustn't*.

Possible answers
If you see snakes / bees / big angry dogs,
… you mustn't go near them.
… you mustn't make them angry.
… you mustn't throw things at them.
… you must stay calm.
… you mustn't touch them.
If you see snakes, you mustn't move or run away.
If you see big dogs, you must walk slowly.

5 🔊 Sing a song. *Flying high, flying low* **10 minutes**

See Pupil's Book page 62 for the words. Show the pupils where they can find the words before playing the recording.

See **A–Z: Songs** on page 91.

ACTIVITY BOOK pages 8 and 9

1 Complete the puzzle. **15 minutes**

Pupils complete the crossword.

Answers

	2			5		7	8	
	B		4	B		S	D	
	U	3	B	E		N	E	
	T	I	I	L		A	S	9
1	T	M	T	O	6	K	E	D
S	O	M	E	W	H	E	R	E
C	N	E			U		T	C
R	D				G			I
E	I				E			D
E	A							E
N	T							
	E					12		
	L				11	S	13	
	Y			10	A	U	J	
				C	P	D	U	
				O	P	D	M	
				D	E	E	P	
				E	A	N	E	
				R	L	D		
				Y				

Suggested answers

3 Gary touched the map
5 It flew very fast over the sea, mountains and forests until they came to a desert.
7 The carpet landed next to a big hole.
9 Suddenly three rattlesnakes appeared.

Answers

2 = b 3 = d 4 = c 5 = e 6 = f 7 = h
8 = a   9 = g

Answers

2 = e 3 = f 4 = c 5 = b 6 = a

2 Look at page 8 in your Pupil's Book. Write sentences to complete the story.   **15 minutes**

Pupils write sentences to complete the story.

3 Read about rattlesnakes. Look at the pictures and write the correct letter in each box.   **20 minutes**

Pupils look at the pictures and write the correct letter in each box.

4 Match the questions and the answers.   **12 minutes**

Pupils match the *Why?* questions with the infinitive of purpose answers.

1B • Language time

Aim
- To practise the grammar and vocabulary from section 1A.

Language
Revision
Zero conditional
Ordinals
New language
afraid, aggressive, away, coral, fossil, hurt, layer, sting, tracks
first, second ... twelfth

What you need
- Cassette / CD and player.

Language time: The B sections provide an opportunity for the pupils to practise the grammar and vocabulary from the A sections.

Before you begin
Sing the song from section 1A.

PUPIL'S BOOK pages 10 and 11

Answer key, tapescript and your notes

1a Read about nature. Can you give some examples of what different animals do?   **10 minutes**

PURPOSE To practise reading and speaking and the zero conditional.

Allow time for pupils to read the text and then either as a whole class, in pairs or groups, to think of specific examples of animal behaviour. They can think about documentaries they have seen on television, things they have seen in the countryside or about their own pets, for example:

If I move suddenly, my guinea pigs run away. If I move slowly and quietly, they don't feel so frightened.

1b Complete the sentences.   **10 minutes**

PURPOSE To practise writing and the zero conditional.

Allow pupils time to write the answers and they can then compare in pairs.

Further practice: Activity Book Exercise 1.

Answers
1 it flies away   2 it jumps
3 it becomes aggressive   4 it hides
5 it swims away   6 it stings you

2 Test your science! Complete the sentences.   **10 minutes**

PURPOSE To practise the zero conditional.

This activity can be done orally or in writing depending on how well the pupils managed the previous exercise. Encourage them to use any language they know.

Further practice: Activity Book Exercise 2.

Suggested answers
1 it falls / breaks   2 it burns   3 it rises
4 it freezes / becomes ice
5 you get cold   6 it goes out

3 Look at the layers of rock in the Grand Canyon. Answer the questions.   **10 minutes**

PURPOSE To introduce or revise ordinal numbers.

Answers
1 The seventh layer is the thinnest.
2 The first layer is the newest.
3 The eleventh layer is the thickest.
4 The twelfth layer is the oldest.

Tapescript

Amy: Max, look at this book about the Grand Canyon. There are lots of fossils there. It says you can find fossils of coral in the first, second and sixth layers of the canyon.

Max: Oh yes. Wow! And look, in the third and fifth layers you can find fossils of animal tracks.

Amy: And plants in the fourth layer.

Max: Yes, and small sea animals in the eighth, ninth and tenth layers.

Amy: And look, there are sea **plants** too in the ninth layer.

Max: What's that in the eleventh layer, Amy?

Amy: It says they're water marks.

Max: Oh, they're strange. Look, there aren't any fossils in the twelfth layer.

Amy: No. That layer is very, very old.

Max: That's really interesting. I want to go there!

Amy: Me, too!

Answers

animal tracks: 3rd and 5th
plants: 4th
small sea animals: 8th, 9th and 10th layers
sea plants: 9th layer
water marks: 11th layer

Answers

3 = 270   4 = 280   5 = 300   6 = 335   7 = 375
8 = 530   9 = 540   10 = 550   11 = 1 billion
12 = 2 billion

Suggested answers

2 it tries to catch it / it kills it / it chases it
3 it eats it / it pulls it / it picks it up
4 it hides in a rock / it smells the air
5 it repeats them
6 it sits in a tree / it flies to its nest
7 it rains
8 it bursts / it explodes
9 it melts
10 they die

Answers

2 fossils   3 fish and coral   4 reptiles
5 mammals   6 the history of Earth
7 mountains   8 volcanoes   9 the stars
10 restaurant

Check first that the pupils understand the ordinal numbers. Allow time for them to look at the diagram. Pupils can work in pairs and ask and answer the questions together before telling the class.

Further practice: Activity Book Exercises 3a and 3b.

4 Listen. Amy and Max are talking about fossils in the Grand Canyon. Write where you find each type of fossil.

12–15 minutes

PURPOSE To practise listening and ordinal numbers.

You may like to play the recording as far as the information about coral and discuss the example with the class. Make sure that everyone understands the abbreviations for the ordinals. Continue with the recording, asking the pupils to take notes of where the other fossils are found.

5 How old are the layers? Copy the table. Work with a friend. One of you is A and the other is B. Take it in turns to say the next smallest number. Complete the table.

12 minutes

PURPOSE To introduce the numbers over 100.

Most pupils will have come across the numbers over 100 in cross-curricular work in their previous years of English. These numbers are introduced here and then given a specific focus in section 2C. If necessary, spend a few minutes practising numbers over 100 on the board. Then ask the pupils to copy the table. Go over the two examples as a class and check that everyone understands what the next smallest number is in each box. In Box A, this is 270 and in Box B, 280.

PAIRWORK Pupils work in pairs and look at the numbers for A or B. They take it in turns to find the next smallest number and to put it into a sentence with the correct ordinal number. They complete their table by writing the numbers in the correct spaces.

ACTIVITY BOOK pages 10 and 11

1 Complete the sentences.   **8 minutes**

Pupils complete the zero conditional sentences.

2 Write 'If ...' sentences about you.   **12 minutes**

Pupils complete and write sentences that are true for them.

3a Read the museum leaflet. Write the label for each room. One description is missing in the leaflet.   **20 minutes**

Pupils read the leaflet and label the rooms, working out which room is not described in the leaflet.

3b Where can you find these things in the museum?   10 minutes

Pupils write phrases with ordinal numbers as in the example.

Answers
2 in the first room   3 in the fifth room
4 in the ninth room   5 in the third room
6 in the seventh room
7 in the second room   8 in the tenth room
9 in the eighth room   10 in the fourth room

1C • Snakes!

Topic

Alice escapes from the hole with the card because James throws stones to distract the snakes. They put the card into the control panel and Gary cracks the code. The carpet zooms off to the next destination.

Aim

- To introduce *too*.

Language

New language
Alice was too frightened to move so she stood very still.

climb, expensive, far away, frightened, high, hole, loud, map, old, push, slow, stone, throw, touch

What you need

- Cassette / CD and player.

Before you begin

Sing the song from section 1A.

PUPIL'S BOOK pages 12 and 13

① 📻 Read and listen. Why is Alice angry with Gary?   **20 minutes**

PURPOSE To practise listening, speaking and reading and to introduce *too*.

LISTENING TO THE STORY Allow time for pupils to look at the pictures before playing the recording. Ask pupils what they can see in each picture and ask them what they know about snakes.

Play the recording and ask the pupils to find the answer to the question *Why is Alice angry with Gary? (Because he always touches the map before the others and doesn't discuss things with them.)*

Ask pupils if they can work out the code to find the next destination *(the Great Wall of China).*

Further practice: Activity Book Exercise 1.

② Read the story again. Put the sentences in the correct order.   **8 minutes**

PURPOSE To help pupils look more closely at the story.

Pupils can work in pairs to read the sentences and put them in the correct order.

Further practice: Activity Book Exercises 2 and 3.

③ Match the parts of the sentences.   **6 minutes**

PURPOSE To practise *too*.

Check that the pupils understand the meaning of *too*. Pupils then match the parts of the sentences.

④ Work with a friend. Fred had a terrible holiday last year. Take turns to follow a line. What was wrong?   **10 minutes**

Answer key and your notes

Answers
c = 1 f = 2 b = 3 d = 4 h = 5 a = 6
e = 7 g = 8

Answers
2 = c 3 = a 4 = b

Suggested answers
The music was too loud / The hotel was too noisy so he couldn't sleep.
The water was too hot so he couldn't wash.
The bed was too short so he couldn't sleep.
The bill was too expensive so he couldn't pay it.
The door was too big so he couldn't close it.
The window was too high so he couldn't open it / close it / see anything.
The / His dinner / meal was too small so he was hungry.
The / His suitcase was too heavy so he couldn't lift / carry it.
The swimming pool was too cold so he couldn't swim.
The room was too dark so he couldn't read.

Check that the pupils understand how to use *too* and look at the use of *couldn't* and the other past tense verbs in Exercise 3. Give them some nouns and adjectives and ask them to think of sentences. You could use:

ice-cream / cold   soup / hot   coat / expensive   shoes / small

Before pupils do the activity, ask them if and where they remember seeing Fred before (Activity Book page 6) and remind them that he was dreaming of what he was going to do on his holiday.

PAIRWORK   Pupils then work in pairs, taking it in turns to follow a line and describe the problems that Fred had on his holiday.

Further practice: Activity Book Exercise 4.

ACTIVITY BOOK pages 12 and 13

1 Find the words. Then match the words and the pictures.   10–15 minutes

Pupils match the words in the puzzle with the pictures.

2 Look at page 12 in your Pupil's Book. Answer the questions.   8 minutes

Pupils read the story again and answer the questions.

3 Complete the story.   12 minutes

Pupils write words to complete the story.

4 Write about Fred's terrible holiday.   12 minutes

Pupils use the phrases in the box to write about Fred's holiday.

Answers

```
C A R P E T E Y R E
M A P O P E P W V N
V G C W U L P K N O
W Q L Z S A L L K L
F R I G H T E N E D
W N M L L H O N E X
Z S B A S R D D S O
S L D G T O U C H U
M O U Y O W P N H U
E W C O N K O R E G
Z W H K E H O L E R
D E F A R   A W A Y
```

Action words: climb throw touch push
Words to describe things: far away frightened old slow
Names of things: map hole stone carpet

Suggested answers

2 He threw stones. 3 He read about them. 4 When they put the card in the control panel. 5 On the screen. 6 Gary.

Answers

2 button 3 control panel 4 window 5 hole 6 rattlesnakes 7 stones 8 snakes 9 heads 10 it 11 code 12 screen 13 map 14 carpet

Suggested answers

2 The bread was too hard so he couldn't eat it.
3 The beach was too dirty so he couldn't sit on it.
4 His camera was too old so he couldn't take pictures.
5 His hat was too big so he couldn't wear it.
6 The hotel was too noisy so he couldn't sleep.

1D • Know it all! The Grand Canyon

Topic
The pupils learn about the Grand Canyon: its formation, history and how this natural spectacle is enjoyed today. They also learn about Yellowstone National Park and how geysers happen. You could have ready more information about the Grand Canyon (for Pupil's Book Exercises 2a and 2b), Yellowstone National Park and geysers (for Activity Book Exercises 1a and 1b) and about old natural places in your country (for the pupils' project).

Project work
Pupils find out and write about a very old natural place in their country.

Language
New language
ago, beauty, canyon, deer, exciting, goat, grow, keep, lizard, raft, special

What you need
• Cassette / CD and player.

Know it all: *In the D sections, the pupils expand their vocabulary by looking at topics which are linked in some way with the story. The topics are also a means to involve pupils in English through a focus on content, allowing them to become 'experts' as they learn from Professor Know It All. They then extend their knowledge by researching for a project linked with the topic of the section. You can encourage pupils to use encyclopaedias and to draw pictures or to find the information and pictures that they need on the Internet. See also **A–Z: Project work** on page 90 and **Content-based language learning** on page 79.*

English Control Panel: *The pupils prepared their English Control Panel in the* Welcome! *unit and at the end of each unit, they complete it with words and sentences as a record of learning (see pages 5 and 7). If any of the pupils didn't use* Primary Colours 4 *or didn't make the Time Travel Journal, you may like to allow class time for them to complete their English Control Panel for the first time so that everyone understands what they have to do.*

Learning skills: *At the end of each unit in the Activity Book, pupils are introduced to different learning strategies for independent practice. In this unit, they are encouraged to make their own exercises to help them practise and revise new vocabulary and grammar. As this is an important part of the learning process, it may be worthwhile making some time in class to discuss the ideas and then to allow time in future lessons to ask whether anyone has made any exercises at home. Pupils can exchange the exercises that they make or they can put them in a file or box so that fast finishers in future lessons can choose an exercise to do in class while the others finish. See **A–Z: Mixed abilities** on page 86.*

Answer key, tapescript and your notes

Answers
1 Answers a, b, c and d are all correct.
2 = d   3 = d   4 = c   5 = d   6 = a

PUPIL'S BOOK pages 14 and 15

1a Look at the pictures and answer the questions. Compare with your friends.   **12 minutes**

PURPOSE To learn about the Grand Canyon.

Allow time for the pupils to look at the pictures and to give you any information they know about the Grand Canyon. Pupils then work alone and answer the questionnaire before comparing with a partner. It does not matter if they are unsure about the answers at this stage as the recording provides the answers in the next exercise.

1b Listen to Professor Know It All. Check your answers.   **15 minutes**

PURPOSE To practise listening intensively.

Pupils listen to the interview and check their answers.

1b Tapescript

Int = Interviewer *Prof* = Professor

Int: Hello! Welcome! And welcome back to Professor Know It All, the man who knows everything! Hello, Professor.

Prof: Hello.

Int: Professor, today we're going to talk about the Grand Canyon. We have some photographs here. It's absolutely fantastic, isn't it?

Prof: Yes, it is really beautiful.

Int: But Professor, why is it like that?

Prof: Well, that's a very difficult question! We think that millions of years ago, the land moved together and made mountains.

Int: Really?

Prof: Yes, it was under the sea then. Then later, the sea moved away and left the mountains. A river, the Colorado River, ran through the mountains and slowly took away a lot of the rock. Also, snow and ice in the winters took away more rock.

Int: Fascinating! So, Professor, can you tell us some facts about the size of the Grand Canyon?

Prof: Yes, of course. It's about 400 kilometres long and about one and a half kilometres deep in some places.

Int: And do any animals live there?

Prof: Oh yes! There are lots of different animals, big and small. There are reptiles, mammals, birds and of course many insects. You can see bats, sheep, deer and mountain lions. They live in the North of the canyon.

Int: How do they live there?

Prof: Well, in the North, it is very green. It rains and in the winter there is snow. There is always water, you see.

Int: And do any people live there?

Prof: Oh yes. We know that people lived there thousands of years ago. There are also small numbers of people who live there today.

Int: Well, thank you, Professor. That's all we have time for today. Goodbye to you all!

Prof: Yes, and goodbye from me!

Further practice: Activity Book Exercises 1a and 1b.

2a Look at these pictures of the Grand Canyon. What do you think they tell us?   **10 minutes**

Allow time for the pupils to look at the pictures of the Grand Canyon and to use their imagination to work out some ideas.

If any pupils have visited the Grand Canyon, encourage them to tell the class about what they saw and experienced when they were there.

2b Read and match the descriptions and the pictures.   **12 minutes**

Answers
a = 4 b = 3 c = 5 d = 2 e = 1

PURPOSE To practise scanning.

Encourage pupils to scan the texts – to read them through quickly with the aim of finding certain information – and then to match the descriptions and the pictures. They should try to pick out key information without being overly concerned about the exact meaning of every word. This is a key reading skill which is developed through this kind of exercise.

Further practice: Activity Book Exercise 2.

Your project

PURPOSE To allow pupils time to develop their own research and writing skills.

Have ready more information about the old natural places in your country from encyclopaedias and the Internet or ask pupils who have Internet access to look at home. Pupils then work alone or in pairs to produce a poster, booklet or PowerPoint presentation about their topic.

See **A–Z: Project work** on page 90.

Answers

2 = d   3 = b   4 = a

Suggested answers

2 Sometimes more than 200°C.
3 Holes in the ground with gas and water.
They are different colours because of the
things under the ground.
4 Trees in a forest.

Answers

2 Deep   3 hot   4 Water   5 rock   6 pushes
7 space   8 go   9 explodes   10 happens

ACTIVITY BOOK pages 14 and 15

New words in Activity Book 1D: alive, geyser, mud, mudpot, petrified, waterfall

1a Read about Yellowstone Park in the USA. Match the texts and the pictures. **15 minutes**

Pupils read and match the texts with the pictures.

1b Answer the questions. **12 minutes**

Pupils read in more detail and answer the questions.

2 How does a geyser happen? Complete the text. **15 minutes**

Pupils complete the text with the words in the box.

Learning skills: Make your own exercises (1)

One of the best ways of helping pupils remember the new words in a unit is to ask them to make vocabulary puzzles or exercises. Making exercises requires cognition and creativity which help long-term understanding instead of short-term memorisation.

Discuss the ideas as a class. Pupils can either try the activities in class or make some exercises for homework. They can swap these with a friend or put them in a file or box in class for fast finishers.

Pupils can make a crossword puzzle with ten words from the unit. They draw the empty boxes for the words, add the numbers and write numbered clues for each word – they can draw a picture, write a definition or provide a translation in their mother tongue.

The other idea is that the pupils copy sentences from the unit and then cut them up into individual words. They then practise putting them in the correct order.

If they make these exercises in class, go round and help. This will be a good way for you to see how much they have understood from the unit and where you may need to provide additional help for individual pupils.

EXTRA IDEA Pupils can also put their exercises into their **portfolio**.

English Control Panel

As this is the first time the pupils complete their English Control Panel, allow class time for discussion and show them your completed model if you have one. Pupils then record the most important vocabulary and grammar from the unit. They compare their words and sentences with a partner and add others if they wish. Allow time for them to ask you questions if they realise that they have not understood something.

EXTRA IDEA Fast finishers can do further work on their project.

EXTRA PRACTICE There are photocopiable *Extra practice* exercises for this unit on pages 96 and 97. The answers are on page 108.

UNIT TEST There are many ways of assessing the pupils' progress (see **A–Z: Assessment** on page 78). If you use formal testing with your class, you may like to use the photocopiable *Test* for this unit on pages 110 and 111. The tapescript and answers are on page 123.

2 A long way from home

2A • Lost in the mist

Topic
Gary, Alice and James are flying through the air with Gary controlling the carpet. The carpet lands in thick mist and they eventually realise that they are at the Great Wall of China. They find the card in the wall but the mist is so thick that they can't find the carpet again.

Aim
• To introduce / revise the past simple and the past continuous.

Language
New language
They looked up the hill.

Gary was sitting near the control panel.

While they were talking, the carpet suddenly went straight up.

add, control, dark, enormous, hill, left, lost, mist, perhaps, point, right, top

What you need
• Cassette / CD and player.

Before you begin
Sing the song from Unit 1.

Ask pupils what they remember about the ending of the story in Unit 1.

PUPIL'S BOOK pages 16 and 17

1 **Read and listen. What problems do the children have now?** 20 minutes

PURPOSE To practise listening, speaking and reading.

LISTENING TO THE STORY Allow time for the pupils to look at the pictures and to try and read the story before playing the recording. This will help with their listening comprehension.

Play the recording and ask pupils to find the answer to the question *What problems do the children have now? (They can't find the carpet in the mist and it's getting dark.)*

Ask pupils to compare their ideas about what the children can do.

Further practice: Activity Book Exercise 1.

2 **Read the story again. Find someone who ...** 7 minutes

PURPOSE To help pupils look more closely at the story.

Pupils work in pairs for this exercise. Remind them that there may be more than one possible answer.

Further practice: Activity Book Exercise 2.

3 **Look at the story again for one minute. Then cover it. Work with a friend. One of you is A and the other is B. Take it in turns to ask and answer.** 12 minutes

PURPOSE To practise asking and answering questions using the past continuous.

Answer key and your notes

Answers
2 Alice and James   3 Gary   4 James
5 James and Gary   6 Alice

Answers
A
1a He was controlling the carpet.
1b She was writing.
2a He was touching / feeling / standing next to the wall.
2b She was sitting on a rock.
B
1a He was sitting on the carpet.
1b It was moving down the hill towards them.
2a He was pointing to the left.
2b He was pointing to the right.

2A • Lost in the mist

PAIRWORK Pupils work in pairs, A and B. They read the story again, looking carefully at the pictures, and then take it in turns to ask each other the questions. Go round listening and help as necessary.

> **Answer**
> Route A

4a Read what James says about the way they came. Is it A or B? 〈 8 minutes 〉

PURPOSE To practise reading intensively.

Pupils read the speech bubble carefully and look at the map. They work out which of the routes (A or B) James is describing.

4b James was wrong! Write the correct way. 〈 10–15 minutes 〉

PURPOSE To practise writing and to practise the past simple.

> **Possible answer**
> First, they crossed the river. Then, they turned right and they went past a small tree. Then they climbed over a wall. They turned left by some rocks. Then they came up this hill.

Make sure everyone understands that the correct route the characters took was not the one that James described in Exercise 4a. Pupils can work in pairs to write a description of the correct route. In pairs, one pupil follows the route in their book while the other checks their text.

Further practice: Activity Book Exercises 3, 4a and 4b.

5 📻 Sing a song. *We were walking in the hills ...* 〈 10 minutes 〉

See Pupil's Book page 62 for the words. Show the pupils where they can find the words before playing the recording.

See **A–Z: Songs** on page 91.

> **Answers**
> 2 lost 3 mist 4 control 5 right 6 left
> 7 hill 8 enormous 9 top 10 dark

ACTIVITY BOOK pages 16 and 17

> **Answers**
> Gary: 1, 9, 2, 7, 4, 12
> James: 6, 3, 10, 8, 5, 11

1 Circle the words. Then match them with the pictures and the sentences. 〈 12 minutes 〉

Pupils find the words in the puzzle and match them with the clues.

> **Suggested answers**
> 2 Alice didn't have an umbrella.
> 3–7 in any order:
> It wasn't raining.
> James wasn't using a mobile phone.
> Gary wasn't sitting on the carpet.
> There wasn't a car.
> There weren't any sheep.

2 Look at page 16 in your Pupil's Book. Six of these sentences are about Gary and six are about James. Write 'G' or 'J'. Then put them in the correct order. 〈 15 minutes 〉

Pupils read the story again and label the sentences. They then list the sentence numbers in the correct order.

3 Think about the story. What's wrong with this picture? 〈 15 minutes 〉

Pupils write negative sentences to say what is wrong with the picture.

> **Answers**
> 1 = B 2 = A

4a Which way? Match the texts and the routes A, B or C on the map. 〈 10 minutes 〉

Pupils read the texts and find the matching routes on the map.

> **Possible answer**
> First, they turned right by a small tree. They climbed over a wall and then crossed a narrow river. They turned right in front of a house and then they turned left and walked behind it. Then they arrived at a wide river.

4b Write the missing text. 〈 10 minutes 〉

Pupils write a similar text to the ones in Exercise 4a to describe route C.

2B • Language time

Aim
- To practise the grammar and vocabulary from section 2A.

Language
New language
Past simple: positive, negative and questions
Past simple (irregular forms): came, flew, found, said, saw, thought, went
cross, distance, donkey

What you need
- Cassette / CD and player.

Before you begin
Sing the song from section 2A.

PUPIL'S BOOK pages 18 and 19

Answer key, tapescript and your notes

1a Think about the story. Match the questions and the answers.   12 minutes

Answers
2 = f 3 = h 4 = e 5 = g 6 = b 7 = c 8 = a

PURPOSE To revise and practise past simple regular and irregular forms.

Use the example to remind the class about irregular past simple forms. You may like to do the activity orally as a class. Alternatively pupils can work first on their own and check in pairs.

1b Find the past of the **verbs** in Exercise 1a. Can you see a pattern? Which group ends in '-ed' to make a past tense?   12 minutes

Answer
Group 1: see – saw   go – went
find – found
Group 2: travel – travelled
discover – discovered   point – pointed
Group 2 ends in '-ed' to make a past tense.

PURPOSE To revise regular and irregular past simple forms.

Pupils copy and complete the verb table in their exercise books and identify the regular '-ed' ending. Discuss their answers.

Further practice: Activity Book Exercise 1a.

2a Imagine that Alice is telling a friend about what happened. Complete the story.   12 minutes

Answers
2 arrived 3 looked 4 said 5 climbed
6 came 7 discovered 8 went 9 found
10 started 11 thought 12 came
13 pointed 14 wanted

Pupils write the numbers 1–14 in their exercise books and complete the story by writing the correct past simple form.

2b Add more verbs to the groups in Exercise 1b.   5–10 minutes

Answers
Group 1: said came thought
Group 2: looked climbed started wanted

Pupils can work alone or in pairs. If time allows, they can look back through all the stories and other reading texts to find more verbs.

Further practice: Activity Book Exercise 1b.

3a What was happening when the children were talking? Work with a friend. Make five sentences.   12–15 minutes

Answers
1 The birds were flying home.
2 The donkey was carrying lots of things.
3 Some sheep were crossing the river.
4 The sun was going down.
5 The mist was moving down the hill.

PURPOSE To practise the past continuous.

PAIRWORK Pupils work in pairs to make five true sentences.

Possible answers

James was pointing to the left.
Gary was pointing to the right.
A boy was walking with a donkey.
The boy was carrying a bag and a lantern.
The moon was shining.
The wind was blowing.
A dog was running behind the sheep.
A goat was eating the grass.

Answers

The birds weren't landing in the trees. They were flying.

The sheep weren't sleeping on the ground. They were crossing the river.

A dog wasn't crossing the river. The sheep were crossing the river. / It was running behind the sheep.

A man wasn't walking with his donkey. A boy was walking with his donkey.

The donkey wasn't walking next to him. It was walking behind him.

The man (boy) wasn't carrying lots of things. The donkey was carrying lots of things.

Answers

2 went   3 arrived   4 saw   5 found
6 discovered   7 thought   8 wanted
9 flew   10 went

Possible answers

2 ate them all   3 went for a bike ride
4 walked by the river   5 saw you

Suggested answers

Jackie was driving her car when a cat jumped on it.

Robert was eating a sandwich when a bird flew down and took it.

Helen was sitting in a café when it started to rain.

Henry was cycling when a banana (skin) landed / fell on his head.

Sue was talking on her mobile phone when she walked into a man.

Tom and Bill were drinking something when a football crashed into them.

Pat and Keith were looking at a shop (window) when water hit them.

3b Can you say more sentences about the picture?   **7 minutes**

PURPOSE   To develop fluency.

Ask pupils to make up more sentences about the picture. Although the focus has been on the past continuous, allow them to give their own ideas using any language they know.

3c   Listen to James. Find six mistakes.   **10 minutes**

PURPOSE   To practise listening intensively and to practise the past continuous negative.

Pupils listen to the recording and make notes about the differences between what they hear and the picture. Elicit their ideas and help them to make sentences using both the past continuous negative and positive.

Tapescript

James: *We were standing near the Great Wall. It was getting very cold. The sun was going down, but the moon was shining in the sky. Some birds were landing in the trees. Some sheep were sleeping on the ground. A dog was crossing the river.*

A man was walking with his donkey. The donkey was walking next to him. The man was carrying lots of things. The mist was moving very quickly. We couldn't see very much!

4 Work with a friend. Ask and answer. Can you think of more questions?   **8 minutes**

PURPOSE   To develop fluency and to practise the past continuous.

PAIRWORK   In pairs, pupils ask and answer the questions and then continue by thinking of more questions. Go round and help and check that they are using the past continuous.

Further practice: Activity Book Exercise 2.

ACTIVITY BOOK pages 18 and 19

1a Max is telling Amy about his weekend. Complete the conversation.   **12 minutes**

Pupils complete the conversation with the correct past simple forms.

1b Now look at the pictures. Complete the rest of the conversation.   **12–15 minutes**

Pupils use the pictures to help them complete the conversation.

2 What happened to these people? Look at the pictures and find the differences.   **15 minutes**

Pupils look at the pictures and write sentences about the differences.

2C • A night in a cave

Topic
The children meet a Chinese boy. Gary surprises Alice and James by answering the boy in Chinese and being able to translate. The boy takes them to a cave nearby where they can sleep. In the morning the mist has cleared and the boy takes them back to the wall, from where they can now see the carpet. Alice cracks the code and touches the map. They fly off on the carpet to their next destination.

Aim
• To introduce the numbers over 100.

Language
New language
Past simple (irregular forms): hid, put, ran, told, took
(six) hundred (and), (seven) thousand (and)
cave, hide, light, put, shout, smile, translate

What you need
• Cassette / CD and player.

Before you begin
Sing the song from section 2A.

PUPIL'S BOOK pages 20 and 21

Answer key, tapescript and your notes

1 **Read and listen. Why isn't Gary interested in the Great Wall?** 20 minutes

PURPOSE To practise listening, speaking and reading.

LISTENING TO THE STORY Allow time for pupils to look at the pictures before playing the recording. Ask pupils what they can see in each picture.

Play the recording and ask the pupils to find the answer to the question *Why isn't Gary interested in the Great Wall? (Because he just wants to find the carpet.)*

Ask pupils if they can work out the code to find the next destination *(Mount Kenya National Park).*

EXTRA IDEA Gary says *Hello* (Ni hao) and *Thank you* (Doh je) in Chinese. Explain if necessary that this is not how Chinese is written. Ask the pupils if they know these words in other languages. Encourage them to share them with the rest of the class and teach the others how to say them. As a follow-up activity you could make a classroom display with a map of the world. Write phrases in a variety of languages in speech bubbles and put them on or near the relevant country.

Further practice: Activity Book Exercise 1.

2 **Read the story again. Who can say these sentences?** 10 minutes

PURPOSE To help pupils look more closely at the story.

Pupils read the story carefully and decide who could say these sentences. To check understanding, you may also like them to say in which picture the character would say them. They compare their answers in a small group and then share them with the class.

Further practice: Activity Book Exercise 2.

Answers
1 James   2 Gary   3 the boy   4 Alice
5 the boy   6 Gary   7 Alice

Tapescript

The Great Wall of China is 650 years old. The wall is 11 metres high. The highest point is 980 metres above the sea. It is 7,200 kilometres long. It is about 7 metres wide. There are towers every 180 metres. There are more than 10,000 towers in total.

Answers

2 11 3 980 4 7,200 5 7 6 180
7 10,000

 3a Look at this information about the Great Wall. Complete the facts.   12 minutes

PURPOSE To practise the numbers over 100.

Allow time for the pupils to look closely at the picture and to read the facts about the Great Wall. They then try to match the numbers with each fact. Ask for their ideas and help with saying any of the bigger numbers as necessary. If the pupils have different ideas, explain that they will hear the answers in the next exercise.

3b Listen and check your answers.   15 minutes

PURPOSE To practise intensive listening.

Play the recording once all the way through. Then play it again, pausing so that the pupils can check their answers.

Note: *Statistics for the wall vary in different sources as changes in technology have enabled archaeologists to revise their estimates. Sources also give different dates for the wall because a much older wall existed before the remains of what we now see today.*

Further practice: Activity Book Exercise 3.

 4a Copy this card twice. Work with a friend. Take it in turns to choose a number from the box. Say it to your friend. Your friend must write it on one of their cards.   8–10 minutes

PURPOSE To practise saying the numbers over 100.

If the numbers over 100 are new for the class, you may like to check that everyone knows how to say the numbers in the box before pupils make their two small bingo cards and move into the pairwork stage.

PAIRWORK Pupils then work in pairs taking it in turns to dictate numbers to their partner. Their partner has to use these numbers to complete their two bingo cards but they can choose which numbers they write on which card.

Tapescript

898 904 456 555 213 475 378 4,000
823 120 982 701 743 123 466 545

4b Listen and play bingo.   5 minutes

There are different ways of using the bingo game but the first option is the most collaborative.

- Pupils work in pairs and only call *Bingo!* when they have each completed one of their cards. This pair (or pairs if more than one pair finish at the same time) are the winners.
- Pupils work in pairs but only play the game 'against' each other to see who completes their two cards first.
- Pupils work on their own and call *Bingo!* when they have completed both their cards.

For further oral practice, they can continue playing in small groups, but pupils who worked together in the pairwork stage should be in different groups. They take it in turns to call out the numbers, keeping a note of the ones they have used.

Further practice: Activity Book Exercises 4, 5a and 5b.

ACTIVITY BOOK pages 20 and 21

1 Find the verbs in Puzzle A. Find the past of the verbs in Puzzle B. | 15 minutes

Pupils circle the infinitive and past simple verb forms for each picture.

Answers

A

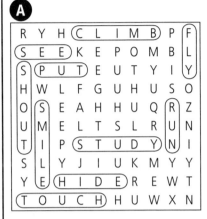

B

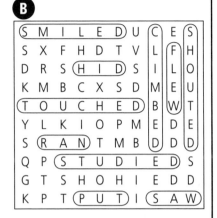

2 hide – hid   3 fly – flew   4 see – saw   5 run – ran   6 touch – touched
7 climb – climbed   8 shout – shouted   9 study – studied   10 smile – smiled

Possible answers
2 We came / travelled / flew on a carpet.
3 We found it in James' attic.
4 We sat on it and touched the control panel.
5 Laya appeared.
6 A girl from another planet.
7 We visit different countries and we have to find a control card.

2 Gary is talking to the Chinese boy. Complete the conversation. Use your own ideas. | 15 minutes

Pupils use their own words to complete Gary's explanation of why they are in China.

3 Draw lines from the words to the numbers. | 10 minutes

Pupils form the numbers shown on the right in words by drawing lines.

Answers
² nine thousand, four hundred and twelve
³ fourteen thousand, three hundred and forty-five
⁴ one thousand, two hundred and ninety
⁵ six hundred and twenty-two
⁶ seven thousand, five hundred and forty-six

4 Write the numbers in words. | 12 minutes

Pupils write out the numbers.

5a Read about the Great Wall of China. Then read the sentences again and complete them with the numbers in words from Exercise 4. | 15 minutes

Encourage the pupils to read the whole text before going back through to complete it with the numbers from Exercise 4. They check their answers in the next exercise.

Answers
b seven hundred
c two hundred and seventy-five
d six hundred and fifty
e three hundred and sixty
f six thousand, four hundred
g two
h one million

5b Check your answers. | 15 minutes

Pupils look at the upside-down answers and check which answer in Exercise 4 matches each gap in the text. They can then check their spelling in Exercise 4.

Answers
b two hundred and seventy-five
c one million
d six thousand, four hundred
e seven hundred
f one ... two
g three hundred and sixty

2D • Know it all! The Great Wall

Topic

The pupils learn more about the building of the Great Wall and read a legend connected with it. You could have ready more information about this topic (for Pupil's Book Exercises 1a and 1b), about the Xi'an soldiers (for Activity Book Exercise 1) and about legends from your country (for the pupils' project).

Project work

The pupils find out and write about an old story from their country.

Language

New language
Past simple (irregular forms): built, did

beautiful, body, build, cry, dead, emperor, hard, marry, soldier, statue, temple

What you need

• Cassette / CD and player.

English Control Panel: Remind pupils to start completing their English Control Panels for Unit 2.

Answer key, tapescript and your notes

PUPIL'S BOOK pages 22 and 23

1a Think about these questions. Tell the class your ideas. **15 minutes**

PURPOSE To learn about the Great Wall of China and share knowledge.

Pupils work in pairs and groups and try and brainstorm some answers to the questions. They can then share their answers in class.

It does not matter if they are unsure about the answers at this stage as the recording provides the answers in the next exercise.

Answers

1 The emperors / kings of China.
2 To keep other people out.
3 Hundreds of years.
4 No, they didn't, because it was very hard work.

1b Listen to Professor Know It All. Check your answers. **12 minutes**

Pupils listen to the interview and check their answers.

Tapescript

Int = Interviewer **Prof** = Professor

Int: Welcome back! And welcome back to Professor Know It All, the man who knows everything! Today, Professor Know It All is going to tell us about the Great Wall of China. Professor, the Great Wall of China is over 600 years old and over 7,000 kilometres long. We know that, but Professor, why did they build it?

Prof: Well, hundreds of years ago, China had a big problem. The people from the next countries were trying to attack them. For this reason, they decided to build an enormous wall. To keep these people out!

Int: Oh, I see. But whose idea was this?

Prof: Well, the emperors – or kings – of China wanted the wall.

Int: Did it take very long to build?

Prof: Oh yes! In fact, hundreds and hundreds of years! One emperor built one part, then another emperor built another part, and so on. Most of the wall that we see today is from about 600 years ago.

Int: Did people want to build the wall?

Prof: I don't know! Probably they wanted a wall, but they didn't want to build it! Many people worked on the wall. The emperors forced them. It was very hard work and many people died while they were working on it. I'm sure it was a terrible job.

Int: Well, thank you very much, Professor. Once again, you are the man who knows it all! So that's goodbye from me and from the Professor.

Prof: Goodbye!

Int: Goodbye!

Answers

1 = g 2 = e 3 = c 4 = a 5 = f 6 = b
7 = d

2 Read the story. Match the parts of the story and the pictures. **15 minutes**

PURPOSE To practise reading.

Pupils work alone to match the texts and the pictures.

The story is recorded as an optional listening element. You may like to play it as the pupils read for the first time, to allow the natural intonation in the recording to help them with comprehension. Alternatively, you may prefer to play it at the end of the exercise.

Further practice: Activity Book Exercises 1 and 2.

Your project

PURPOSE To allow pupils time to develop their own research and writing skills.

Have ready more information about legends and myths from your country and / or your pupils' countries from encyclopaedias and websites or ask pupils to look if they have access to the Internet. Pupils then work alone or in pairs to produce a story. This can be a booklet, a PowerPoint presentation or a story in the form of a cartoon strip.

FOLLOW UP Leave time in a future lesson for the pupils to display and discuss their stories. They can then also be included in each pupil's **portfolio.**

ACTIVITY BOOK pages 22 and 23

New vocabulary in Activity Book 2D: attack, fight, guard, model, ready, unfortunately

1 Read about the Xi'an soldiers. What are each of these numbers about? **10 minutes**

Pupils scan the text to find what each number refers to.

2 In 2006, another 'soldier' wanted to join the Xi'an soldiers! Complete the text. **15 minutes**

Pupils complete the text with the correct form of the verbs.

Learning skills: Make your own exercises (2)

Discuss the ideas as a class. Pupils can either try the activities in class or make some exercises for homework. They can swap these with a friend or put them in a file or box in class for fast finishers.

Pupils can write out words with meanings or pictures and then cut off the meaning or picture to practise matching them.

The other idea is that the pupils make anagrams and put them away for at least a day before using them to practise.

If they make these exercises in class, go round and help. This will show you how much they have understood and where you may need to provide additional help for individual pupils.

English Control Panel

Check that the pupils have completed their English Control Panel for Unit 2, whether in class or at home.

EXTRA IDEA Fast finishers can do further work on their project.

EXTRA PRACTICE There are photocopiable *Extra practice* exercises for this unit on pages 98 and 99. The answers are on page 108.

UNIT TEST There is a photocopiable *Test* for this unit on pages 112 and 113. The tapescript and answers are on page 123.

Answers
2 model soldiers
3 years ago when Qin was emperor
4 when Qin became emperor
5 people who made the soldiers
6 years to make the soldiers
7 horses

Answers
2 made 3 went 4 jumped 5 stood
6 saw 7 pointed 8 took 9 came
10 wanted

Revision

Topic
This section contains revision exercises.

Aim
- To revise the language covered in Units 1 and 2.

Language
Revision
Ordinal numbers
Numbers over 100
Past simple and past continuous
Infinitive of purpose
New language
Past simple (irregular forms): had, lost
hunt, joke, type

What you need
- Cassette / CD and player.

Revision and evaluation: There are revision sections in the Pupil's Book and Activity Book after Units 2, 4 and 6. The Revision and evaluation section in the Activity Book begins by asking pupils to reflect on how well they can remember the new language of the previous two units. Encourage them to look back through their Pupil's Books, Activity Books and English Control Panels to refresh their memory. As this is the first revision unit in the book, you may want to allow time in class for pupils to complete this section. In subsequent revision units, this and most of the other exercises could be set as homework if you prefer. See **A–Z: Evaluation** *on page 83.*

Answer key, tapescript and your notes

Answers

2 They go climbing on the second, fifth and seventh days of the trip.

3 They are free on the third and ninth mornings and the fifth, eighth and tenth afternoons.

4 They go rafting on the fourth and eighth days of the trip.

5 They go walking on the second and tenth days of the trip.

6 They listen to talks on the history of the canyon on the third, seventh and ninth days of the trip.

7 They hunt for fossils on the fourth and sixth days of the trip.

8 They watch a film about the canyon on the first day of the trip.

PUPIL'S BOOK pages 24 and 25

1 Look at the information about a trip to the Grand Canyon. Answer the questions.   **12 minutes**

PURPOSE To revise ordinal numbers.

Pupils can work in pairs to read and answer the questions.

Note: *We suggest that the pupils work on relevant Activity Book exercises after completing their self-evaluation (see page 30).*

Further practice: Activity Book Exercise 2.

2a Listen to more information about the Grand Canyon. Write the missing numbers.   **10 minutes**

PURPOSE To practise listening intensively.

Play the recording once straight through. Play it again, pausing so that pupils can write the numbers. Pupils check their answers in the following exercise as oral pairwork.

> **Tapescript**
>
> *Facts about the Grand Canyon:*
> *The Grand Canyon is very deep.*
> *The lowest point is 1,525 metres above the sea, and the highest point is 2,795 metres above the sea.*
> *There are over 640 kilometres of paths where you can walk.*
> *Today, about 1,460 people live in the Grand Canyon.*
>
> *The Colorado River runs through the Grand Canyon. It is 2,333 kilometres long. Inside the Grand Canyon, the river is 444 kilometres long.*
> *There are 287 types of birds, 88 types of mammals, 26 types of fish, 58 types of reptiles and 1,500 types of plants in the Grand Canyon.*

2b Work with a friend. Take it in turns to read a sentence aloud. Check your answers. **8 minutes**

PURPOSE To practise speaking and listening to numbers.

PAIRWORK Pupils work in pairs taking it in turns to say sentences to each other. In doing so, they check their answers to Exercise 2a.

Further practice: Activity Book Exercise 3.

 3a Read the story about a Chinese emperor and his tower on the Great Wall. Choose the correct word or write the correct form of the verb. **20 minutes**

PURPOSE To practise reading and to revise the past simple and the past continuous.

Pupils write the numbers 1–20 in their exercise books and write the correct verb form for each gap.

 3b Listen and check your answers. **15 minutes**

Play the recording all through once for students to get the main idea. Then play it through again pausing at the end of each paragraph and checking any spelling questions the pupils may have.

Further practice: Activity Book Exercise 4.

 4 Where can you add these words to the story? **15 minutes**

PURPOSE To practise reading intensively.

Pupils work alone and look back at the text to try and find logical places for the four phrases. Ask them to write the sentences in their exercise books and then to compare with a partner. If they have different answers, ask them to read them out to the class.

Further practice: Activity Book Exercise 5.

Answers

2 2,795   3 640   4 1,460   5 2,333
6 444   7 287   8 88   9 26   10 58
11 1,500

Tapescript

About 2,000 years ago, there was an emperor called Emperor You. The people in the next country were trying to attack his country, so the emperor built a big tower, with a place for a big fire. 'If they come, we can light the fire,' he said. 'My soldiers must come if they see the fire!'
Emperor You's wife, Bao Si, was always very unhappy. He tried to make her happy, but she never smiled. Then one day, he had an idea. He took her to the tower and told a soldier to light the fire. Immediately, the soldiers ran to the tower and they saw the emperor and Bao Si there. The emperor was laughing at them. 'I was joking!' he said. 'There isn't any danger!' Bao Si thought it was very funny. At last, she was smiling! The emperor did this many times. Each time, the soldiers saw the same thing. The emperor and Bao Si were laughing at them. One day, the people from the next country really attacked when all the emperor's soldiers were sleeping. Immediately, the emperor said, 'Light the fire!' but his soldiers didn't come. They said, 'It's only a joke,' and so Emperor You lost everything.

Answers

3 said   4 tried   5 smiled   6 had   7 took
8 told   9 ran   10 saw   11 was laughing
12 was joking   13 thought   14 was smiling
15 did   16 saw   17 were laughing
18 attacked   19 were sleeping   20 said

Answers

1 Emperor You's wife, Bao Si, was always very unhappy because she wanted to go back to her parents.
2 The people in the next country were trying to attack his country because they wanted the emperor's land.
3 Immediately the emperor said, 'Light the fire!' but his soldiers didn't come because they didn't believe that there was a problem.
4 The emperor did this many times because his wife thought it was very funny.

Answers

2 It's the sixth highest.
3 It's the eighth highest.
4 It's the fourth highest.
5 It's the tenth highest.
7 The third highest.
8 The ninth highest.

Answers

2 It's eight thousand and ninety-one metres.
3 It's eight thousand, five hundred and sixteen metres.
4 It's eight thousand, six hundred and eleven metres.

Answers

3 saw 4 was walking 5 was carrying
6 climbed 7 came 8 saw 9 shouted
10 disappeared 11 arrived 12 found
13 were hiding 14 said 15 answered
16 talked 17 told 18 were trying
19 wanted 20 took

Answers

2 = d 3 = a 4 = c 5 = f 6 = b

ACTIVITY BOOK pages 24 and 25

1 How well can you remember your English? Put a cross ✗ on the arrow. **8 minutes**

If all your pupils worked with *Primary Colours 4*, they will be familiar with the idea of self-evaluation. For some pupils or classes, this may be the first time that they have to think about their learning in this way. Allow some time in class for everyone to do Exercise 1 and explain to the pupils why this kind of self-evaluation is so important and how it can help them.

This activity gives the pupils an opportunity to reflect on their language understanding and progress in the previous two units. Encourage them to spend some time individually thinking about how well they remember each language item in the chart and encourage them to put a cross somewhere along the arrow accordingly. They then start with the exercise which gives them more practice in the area where they feel weakest:

say 'first, second, third', etc.: Exercise 2

say and write the numbers over 100: Exercise 3

describe what was happening: Exercise 4

give a reason for something: Exercise 5

To give the pupils a greater feeling of independence, you could write the answers to exercises in this section on the board, on an overhead transparency or prepare them to project from the computer.

2 Look at the table. Answer the questions. **15–20 minutes**

Pupils write sentences or phrases with ordinals to answer the questions.

3 Look at the table again. Answer the questions. **12 minutes**

Pupils answer the questions by writing out the numbers in words.

4 The Chinese boy is talking to his father about what happened. Choose the correct word or write the correct form of the verb. **15 minutes**

Pupils complete the conversation.

5 Match the questions and the answers. **8 minutes**

Pupils match the questions with the answers.

3 On the mountain

3A • Crash!

Topic

Gary, Alice and James arrive on the carpet over the savannah of Africa and see lots of wild animals. The carpet suddenly starts climbing up, Gary can no longer control it and they crash into the side of Mount Kenya. The children fall off the carpet and manage to hold on to a rock at the edge to stop themselves falling, but the carpet is about ten metres below them.

Aims

- To introduce the future simple (see **Note** on page 33).
- To revise *because*.

Language

Revision
because

New language
When will we get there?
I think we'll land in a few minutes.
You won't feel hot there.
Past simple (irregular forms): fell, hit
grab, ice, land, mountain, rock, savannah, slide, snow, speed

What you need

- Cassette / CD and player.

Before you begin

Sing the song from Unit 2.

Ask pupils what they remember about the ending of the story in Unit 2.

PUPIL'S BOOK pages 26 and 27

1 📻 Read and listen. Why is James frightened? **20 minutes**

PURPOSE To practise listening, speaking and reading.

LISTENING TO THE STORY Allow time for the pupils to look at the pictures and to try and read the story before playing the recording. This will help with their listening comprehension.

Play the recording and ask pupils to find the answer to the question *Why is James frightened? (He thinks they will die on the mountain because they can't get the carpet back.)*

Ask pupils to share their ideas about how they can get the carpet back.

Further practice: Activity Book Exercise 1.

2 Read the story again. Complete the sentences. **10 minutes**

PURPOSE To help pupils look more closely at the story and to revise *because*.

Pupils work alone for this exercise and then compare answers in pairs.

Further practice: Activity Book Exercises 2 and 3.

Answer key and your notes

Suggested answers
2 Laya said, 'Go to somewhere hot then climb'.
3 Mount Kenya is over 5,000 metres high / she can see snow.
4 it / the carpet crashed into the mountain.
5 they grabbed on to a rock.
6 it is ten metres below them.

Answers

On the savannah: 1 = a   2 = c   3 = b
4 = c   5 = d
In the mountains: 6 = d   7 = b   8 = c
9 = d   10 = a

Answers

grab = 4   slide = 3   speed = 9   snow = 8
land = 2   ice = 5   rock = 6   mountain = 1

Answers

2 Alice   3 Gary   4 Alice   5 Alice   6 Gary
7 Alice   8 James

Possible answers

James: We'll die up here.
Alice: We won't get the carpet / home.
Gary: We'll think of a plan.

Answers

Habitat: Africa, savannah
Food: plants, grass   Live for: 18–22 years
Baby: 1 m, 35 kg,
stand and walk immediately
Adult: 1.2 m, 2.3 m long, 50 kg
Top speed: 60 km/hour
How do they hide?: they stand together
Problems: people kill them for their meat
and their skin
Lions are members of the cat family. They
live in Africa and Asia, on the savannah.
Lions only eat meat. Baby lions are about
1.5 kg and 20–25 cm tall. They are blind
and cannot walk. Adult lions grow to about
1 m tall and about 2 m long and weigh
about 160 kg. They live for about 15 to 20
years. They can run very fast – up to about
55 km an hour. Their skin colour is the
same colour as grass. The biggest problem
for lions is that their habitat in Asia is
disappearing.

3a Work with a friend. Take it in turns to choose 'savannah' or 'mountains'. Your friend asks you a question. Write down your answer.   **15 minutes**

Before putting the pupils into pairs, explain that they are going to take it in turns to choose a category, but that their partner will then choose a question for them to answer. Emphasise that the question numbers are only for reference and that they don't have to ask them in order.

PAIRWORK Pupils then work in pairs, asking and making a note of their answers, which they will then check in the next exercise.

3b Check your answers on page 62.   **5 minutes**

Pupils continue working in pairs and check their answers on page 62 (given opposite for your reference). Discuss any answers that surprised the class and encourage them with how much they already knew.

Further practice: Activity Book Exercise 4.

4 Sing a song. *Where can we go today?*   **10 minutes**

See Pupil's Book page 63 for the words. Show the pupils where they can find the words before playing the recording.

See **A–Z: Songs** on page 91.

ACTIVITY BOOK pages 26 and 27

1 Match the parts of the words. Then match the words with the pictures.   **12–15 minutes**

Pupils join the words and match them with the pictures.

2 Look at page 26 in your Pupil's Book. Write the names.   **10–15 minutes**

Pupils read the story again and write the names.

3 The children are on the mountain. Write what they are thinking.   **8 minutes**

Pupils complete the speech bubbles with their own ideas.

4 Read about zebras and complete the table. Then read the table and write about lions.   **20–25 minutes**

Pupils complete the table with notes about zebras. They then read the notes about lions and write about them.

3B • Language time

Aim
- To practise the grammar and vocabulary from section 3A.

Language
Revision
because

New language
Future simple

batteries, coat, guide book, sleeping bag, stove, tent, torch

What you need
- Cassette / CD and player.

Before you begin
Sing the song from section 3A.

PUPIL'S BOOK pages 28 and 29

 1 Read the story again. How many true sentences can you make? | 15 minutes

PURPOSE To practise the future simple.

Note: Pupils who completed Primary Colours 4 *will have met the future simple briefly at the end of the book, to talk about predictions. They also already know the* going to *future, to talk about a pre-planned intention, for example I'm going to play basketball with my friends this afternoon. The future simple talks about something that we feel will definitely happen or is likely to happen, for example I think we'll land soon or We'll never get it back.*

We also use the future simple to make an offer, for example I'll do it for you, but this is not the focus here.

Pupils can work alone or in pairs. They look at the two columns and make true sentences about the story, either by drawing lines or by writing numbers and letters in their exercise books. Their answers may vary as some combinations are true but not necessarily stated in the story. For example, James may think they'll die up there because it is cold in the mountains, but he doesn't say this. Allow plenty of class discussion for fluency practice.

Further practice: Activity Book Exercise 1.

  2a Max is talking to Amy. Listen and answer the questions. | 12–15 minutes

PURPOSE To practise listening intensively and to practise the future simple.

Allow time for pupils to read the questions before playing the recording. Play the recording all through once first and then again pausing it to allow time for the pupils to make notes. For feedback, the pupils can either give natural short answers or you may prefer to elicit full sentences in the future simple.

Answer key, tapescript and your notes

Suggested answers

Alice thinks they'll land in a few minutes because ...
she can see lots of animals from the air.
she can see the savannah.
Alice thinks they'll see more animals on the ground because ...
she can see lots of animals from the air.
she can see the savannah.
James thinks they won't land now because they are going up, not down.
Alice thinks James will feel cold because ...
it is cold in the mountains.
they are going up, not down.
James thinks they'll never get the carpet back because ...
they can't get down.
it is too far away from them.
James thinks they'll die up there because ...
they can't get down.
it is too far away from them.
Gary thinks they won't die up there because they'll think of a plan.

2a Answers

1 (She'll stay) in a tent.
2 (She'll stay there) ten days.
3 (She'll) walk to different places.
4 (She'll eat) dry food in packets.
5 (She'll) talk to her family.

Suggested answers

She'll take a coat because it'll be cold in the mountains.

She'll take batteries because she'll need them for the torch. / She won't take batteries because she won't have her CD player.

She'll take a stove because she can cook her food.

She'll take a torch because it'll be dark at night.

She'll take a sleeping bag because it'll be cold at night.

She won't take a guide book because her brother knows the mountains.

She won't take a CD player because she'll talk to her family.

She won't take a mobile phone because it won't work.

She won't take a bed because she'll sleep on the ground.

Answers

1 Lucy's going to the jungle.
2 Jack's going to the mountains.
3 Sally's going to the desert.

2a Tapescript

Max: Hi, Amy. What are you doing?
Amy: I'm making a list of things I'll need next weekend. My family is going to the mountains. It'll be great fun!
Max: What! Where will you stay?
Amy: Well, I think we'll sleep in a tent.
Max: Oh no. You'll be cold!
Amy: No, we won't. We've got really warm sleeping bags.
Max: How can you carry your camp beds?
Amy: Beds?! We won't need beds! We'll sleep on the ground.
Max: What! How long will you stay there?
Amy: I don't know. Ten days, I think.
Max: Ten days! That's a long time. What will you do?
Amy: Well, I think we'll walk to different places in the mountains.
Max: That's a lot of work! Will you take a guide book?
Amy: No, we've got a map and my brother knows the way. He went there last summer.
Max: What will you eat?
Amy: We'll take lots of dry food in packets. We'll cook it on a stove.
Max: Ergh! Yuck! What else will you do, for example in the evenings when it's dark? How will you play your CD player? Will you take lots of batteries?
Amy: Batteries? I won't take a CD player! I'll talk to my family!
Max: And no TV? Well, I hope you'll be OK! Will you take a mobile phone? Can I call you?
Amy: No! Ha, ha! It won't work in the mountains! Max …
Max: Yes?
Amy: Do you want to come with us?
Max: Er … oh … er … Can I think about it?
Amy: Ha, ha! OK!

2b Look at the picture. Write about what Amy will take and what she won't take. Give a reason. **15 minutes**

PURPOSE To practise writing and the future simple.

Pupils can work alone and then compare answers in pairs. They write sentences as in the model. Allow class discussion if there are differing ideas.

Further practice: Activity Book Exercise 2.

3a Look at the pictures. Guess where these people are going. **10 minutes**

PURPOSE To practise speaking and the future simple.

Allow time for pupils to look at the pictures and to read the speech bubbles. They compare ideas with a partner. Ask volunteers to say where the three people are going.

3b Work with a friend. Take it in turns to choose a place. Talk about what you will or won't see, hear or feel. **10 minutes**

PURPOSE To develop fluency with the future simple.

PAIRWORK Pupils work in pairs, taking it in turns to say one of the places in Exercise 3a. Their partner then has to describe what they will experience, using the expressions in the speech bubbles.

Further practice: Activity Book Exercise 3.

4a Imagine that you are going to an unusual place. Copy the table. Complete the 'My trip' column. **12 minutes**

Allow them time to think of an unusual place. This can be done as a whole class by brainstorming ideas and writing them on the board. Pupils then copy the chart and complete the 'My trip' column, thinking about any of the places from the board or another idea that occurs to them.

4b Work with a friend. Ask and answer. Complete the 'My friend's trip' column. **15 minutes**

PURPOSE To develop fluency with the future simple.

PAIRWORK Pupils now work in pairs and take it in turns to share their ideas and complete the chart. Go round and help with vocabulary.

EXTRA IDEA Ask them to draw a picture or find a photo of the place that they chose and to write some sentences about what they will do on their imaginary trip. This can then go in each pupil's **portfolio**.

Further practice: Activity Book Exercise 4.

ACTIVITY BOOK pages 28 and 29

1 Jack is travelling around the world. What will he see or do in each country? Think about: places, buildings, animals, activities, your own ideas. **15 minutes**

Pupils write future simple sentences with their own ideas. The possible answers opposite are simply ideas you can offer to start the class thinking.

2 Imagine that you're going on a world trip. Draw a line on the map. What will you see and do? **15 minutes**

Pupils plot their own trip on the map in Exercise 1, adding extra countries if they wish. They then write sentences about what they will see and do. Remind them that they should do different things from Jack if they visit the same country.

3 Sam is going to the mountains. Match the questions and the answers. Write the missing questions. **15 minutes**

Pupils match the questions and answers and write the missing questions for the answers given.

4 Sam is talking to Lucy about what he won't be able to do. Complete the conversation. **12 minutes**

Pupils complete the conversation about Sam's camping trip using *won't be able*. They can then practise reading it in pairs.

Possible answers

USA: see yellow taxis / visit the Empire State Building
Peru: visit Machu Picchu / learn Spanish
UK: go to London / eat fish and chips
Egypt: see the pyramids / ride on a camel
Kenya: climb Mount Kenya / see lots of animals
China: see the Great Wall / eat Chinese food
Australia: go to the desert / see kangaroos

Answers

2 = c 3 = d 4 = b 5 = f
6 What will he eat? = e
7 Where will he sleep / stay? = a

Suggested answers

2 you won't be able to have a shower / bath
3 you won't be able to talk to them
4 won't be able to listen to music
5 So you won't be able to send emails
6 you won't be able to sleep very well

3C • Don't move!

Topic

Gary gets the next control card and then Alice sees a rope. She uses the rope to climb down to the carpet and flies back up to James and Gary on it. Laya appears and gives them a new code. Gary cracks the code and the carpet flies off again.

Aim

• To introduce the first conditional.

Language

New language

If I climb down to the carpet, I'll be able to put the card in.

break, brilliant, chance, clue, idea, rope, scary, silence, tale, wet

What you need

• Cassette / CD and player.

Before you begin

Sing the song from section 3A.

Answer key and your notes

Answers

3 crashed   4 mountain(s)   5 fell   6 landed
7 snow   8 went   9 grabbed
10 control card   11 saw   12 rope
13 climbed   14 put   15 control panel
16 flew

Answers

2 If we jump, we'll break our legs.
3 If we get snow on the control card, it won't work.
4 If it gets dark, we won't see anything.
5 If we shout for help, nobody will hear us.
6 If we stay here, we'll die of cold.
7 If I move slowly, I'll be able to get the card.
8 If I get the card, we'll only have one problem.
9 If I ask James to get it, he'll say no.

PUPIL'S BOOK pages 30 and 31

1 **Read and listen. Why does James think that Alice is crazy?** 20 minutes

PURPOSE To practise listening, speaking and reading.

LISTENING TO THE STORY Allow time for pupils to look at the pictures before playing the recording. Ask pupils what they can see in each picture.

Play the recording and ask pupils to find the answer to the question *Why does James think that Alice is crazy? (Because the rope is very old and it could break.)*

Ask pupils if they can work out the code to find the next destination *(Venice)*.

Further practice: Activity Book Exercise 1.

2 **What happened in 3A and 3C? Complete the story.** 12 minutes

PURPOSE To help pupils look more closely at the story.

Pupils work alone. They write the numbers 1–16 in their exercise books and then write the missing words and verb forms. They can check their answers with a partner before finally comparing with the stories on pages 26 and 30.

Further practice: Activity Book Exercise 2.

3 **What were they thinking on the mountain? Complete the sentences.** 12–15 minutes

PURPOSE To practise the first conditional.

Allow time for the pupils to read the thought bubbles. They can work alone or in pairs for this exercise. They match the thought bubble phrases with those in the box and then say them to each other.

EXTRA IDEA Fast finishers can draw and write other thought bubbles.

4 You are at point X. How can you cross the river? What are the dangers? 20 minutes

PURPOSE To practise speaking with the first conditional.

Ask pupils to look carefully at the picture and to think of how they can cross the river and what the dangers are. Demonstrate that you would like them to use the first conditional by completing the models with the class, for example *If I stay here, the bear will eat me.*

GROUPWORK In small groups, pupils make up sentences about the dangers and about how they can get across. Go round and help, allowing all their ideas. Bring the activity to a close by asking volunteers from each group to give some examples first of the dangers and then of how they managed to cross the river.

Further practice: Activity Book Exercises 3a and 3b.

ACTIVITY BOOK pages 30 and 31

1 Complete the puzzle. 12 minutes

Pupils complete the crossword.

2 Look at pages 26 and 30 in your Pupil's Book. Answer the questions. 15 minutes

Pupils read the stories again and answer the questions.

3a Some people are on a cliff in the jungle. They need help. You want to get to them but it's dangerous. Find 'You're here' on the map and write about the dangers. 15–20 minutes

Pupils write first conditional sentences about the dangers on the map.

3b Find a way to get to the people. Write about how you can do it. 15–20 minutes

Pupils study the map and work out how they can reach the people. They write sentences to explain how to do it.

Suggested answers

If I climb the tree, it'll break.
If I walk on the stones, I'll fall because there's ice.
If I use the bridge, I'll fall in.
If I use the boat, it'll sink / won't float.

How to cross the river:

If I put wood on the stones, I'll be able to cross the river.

Answers

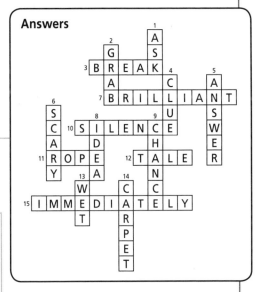

Answers

2 The savannah.   3 They grabbed on to a rock.   4 Ten metres below them.
5 He moved slowly around the rock.
6 She climbed down a rope.

Possible answers

If I use the old helicopter, it'll crash.
If I swim in the river, the crocodiles will eat me.
If I climb the tree, the tree snakes will attack me.
If I walk on the bridge, I'll fall in.

Suggested answer

If I take the left path, I'll be able to jump over the narrow canyon. If I put wood over the big hole, I'll be able to get across. If I walk on the tree, I'll be able to get to the rocks. If I climb the rocks, I'll be able to get to the rope. If I go down the rope, I'll be able to get to the rope on the cliff. If I can get to the rope on the cliff, I'll be able to climb up.

3D • Know it all! Mount Kenya

Topic

The pupils learn about the animals and plants that live in Mount Kenya National Park and in particular about how altitude affects biodiversity. You could have ready more information about this topic (for Pupil's Book Exercises 1, 2a and 3a), about the equator in general (for Activity Book Exercises 1b and 2) and about other famous mountains (for the pupils' project).

Project work

The pupils find out and write about a famous mountain.

Language

New language

bamboo, climate, countryside, eagle, forest, hyena, hyrax, leopard, level, lobelia

What you need

• Cassette / CD and player.

English Control Panel: *Remind pupils to start completing their English Control Panels for Unit 3.*

Learning skills: *The remaining four units offer a different strategy for practising one of the four language skills. The focus in this unit is on speaking. Ideally, pupils would do the activity at home, recording themselves if possible, but you may like to allow time in class to discuss the idea first. In a later lesson you could let those without a means of recording themselves at home do so in class if possible.*

Answer key, tapescript and your notes

Answers

1 elephants (and pupils' own ideas)
2 bamboo, grass, shrubs, trees
3 hot with lots of rain
4 very different – snow, ice and rocks, small trees and rocks, rainforest and bamboo forest

PUPIL'S BOOK pages 32 and 33

1 Mount Kenya National Park is in Africa, near the equator. Look at the pictures. Read the questions and tell the class your ideas.   **15 minutes**

PURPOSE To transfer other subject skills into the English classroom (evidence from a photo) and to share knowledge.

Pupils can work in pairs and groups. They look closely at the pictures and try and brainstorm some answers to the questions. They can then share their answers in class. The pupils won't know the words for everything in the photos and will learn in more detail in later exercises, but suggested answers for you to discuss with the class are given opposite.

2a Do you think these sentences are true or false? Compare with your friends.   **10 minutes**

Allow time for pupils to read and think about the questions. You may want to set this up as a discussion activity in small groups. At this stage it doesn't matter if they are unsure about the answers as they will be checked in the recording in the next exercise.

2b Listen to Professor Know It All. Check your answers.   **12 minutes**

PURPOSE To practise listening intensively.

Play the recording all the way through once and then play it again, pausing at the * given in the tapescript so pupils can check their answers. If pupils worked in groups, you could make it a competition and award points for correct answers.

2b Tapescript

Int = *Interviewer*   *Prof* = *Professor*

Int: *Hello again! And welcome back to Professor Know It All, the man who knows everything! Today, Professor Know It All is going to tell us all about Mount Kenya, one of the biggest mountains in Africa. Professor, what can you tell us?*

Prof: *Well, there's a lot to say! What do you want to know?*

Int: *Well, first of all, where did Mount Kenya come from? I know that millions of years ago, some land crashed together and that pushed up mountains. Is that where Mount Kenya comes from?*

Prof: *Oh no!* It's true that many mountains happened like that, but not Mount Kenya! Mount Kenya is really a volcano!*

Int: *Wow! It's a volcano!*

Prof: *Yes, millions of years ago hot lava came out of the ground and built up a mountain.**

Int: *So is it hot at the top of Mount Kenya?*

Prof: *Oh no! It's a dead volcano, of course! It was active about two and a half million years ago, and it's safe now!**

Int: *But Professor, it doesn't look like a volcano. It doesn't have the shape of a volcano.*

Prof: *No, that's interesting, isn't it? At the top of the mountain, there are eleven very big glaciers. Glaciers are made of ice and they move very slowly.*

Int: *They move?*

Prof: *Yes, the glaciers move very slowly. They are very big and very heavy so, as they move, they take away a lot of the rock.*

Int: *OK, I understand.*

Prof: *And millions of years ago, the glaciers took away the walls of the volcano. That's why Mount Kenya doesn't look like a volcano now.*

Int: *So if there are glaciers at the top, that means it's very cold there.*

Prof: *Oh yes, very cold. At the bottom, it is hot and sunny, but at the top, there is always snow!* In fact, it is so cold that nothing can live up there.**

Int: *Well, I hope I can go to Mount Kenya one day! But today, that's all we have time for. So thank you, Professor. And it's goodbye from us!*

Prof: *Goodbye!*

Further practice: Activity Book Exercises 1a and 1b.

3a Read about the park. Answer the questions.   10 minutes

PURPOSE To practise scanning.

Ask the pupils to scan the text – to read it through quickly with the aim of finding certain information – to find the answers to the questions as quickly as they can. As soon as they have written the answers in their exercise books, they close their books. Make a note of the time on the board.

3b Read the text again. Find an animal or plant which …   10 minutes

PURPOSE To practise reading.

Allow time for pupils to read the text in more detail. They compare their answers with a partner.

Further practice: Activity Book Exercise 2.

Your project

PURPOSE To allow pupils time to develop their own research and writing skills.

Have ready more information about other mountains, some in and some outside the country where your pupils live. This could be from encyclopaedias and websites or you could ask pupils to look if they

---

2b Answers
1 False   2 True   3 False   4 False   5 True
6 True

Answers
1 Below 2,800 metres
2 From 3,000 metres to near the top
3 From 2,800 to near the top
4 Ice, snow and rock, and birds in the sky

Answers
2 bamboo   3 a hyrax   4 a leopard
5 a giant lobelia   6 an eagle

have access to the Internet. Pupils then work alone to produce a poster or other form of presentation about their mountain.

FOLLOW UP Make time in another lesson for the pupils to see each other's work and to talk about it. The work, or a photo of it if it is a large poster, can be put in each child's **portfolio**. If a mountain in your country has a visitors' centre, you could ask whether they would like a copy to add to their display.

See **A–Z: Project work** on page 90.

ACTIVITY BOOK pages 32 and 33

New vocabulary in Activity Book 3D: climate, north, season, south, sunlight, untrue, zero

> **1a** The equator is a line that goes round the middle of the Earth. Read the ideas and circle the correct answers. | 10 minutes

Pupils read what people say about the equator and choose the answer they think is correct. They will check their answers in the next exercise.

> **1b** Read about the equator. Check your answers. | 15 minutes

Pupils read the text and check their answers. Go over the answers as a class and discuss any that pupils are unsure about.

Note: If necessary, explain that 'climate' is not the same as 'season'. Countries on the equator have similar seasons, as the pupils will discover in this section, but the climates within the countries vary, as explained in the penultimate paragraph.

Answers
1 = c   2 = b   3 = b   4 = a

> **2** Answer the questions. Then compare with the information about the equator on page 63. | 12 minutes

Pupils write true answers for where they live and then compare with the information box on page 63.

Learning skills: Speaking

See the note on page 38. Pupils can do this activity at home, but it is useful to allow time in class to discuss the idea first. Check whether everyone is able to record themselves at home and, if not, you may like to set aside a lesson for some pupils to do this in class if you have recording equipment in your school.

Encourage the pupils to use this strategy to practise on their own and ask them from time to time whether they have tried it at home.

English Control Panel

Check that the pupils have completed their English Control Panel for Unit 3, whether in class or at home.

EXTRA IDEA Fast finishers can do further work on their project.

EXTRA PRACTICE There are photocopiable *Extra practice* exercises for this unit on pages 100 and 101. The answers are on page 108.

UNIT TEST There is a photocopiable *Test* for this unit on pages 114 and 115. The tapescript and answers are on page 124.

4A • Where's the carpet?

Topic

Gary, Alice and James arrive on the carpet in a big square in Venice, in Italy. Alice suggests they look for the card in a card shop. James finds the control card on the wall next to the card shop. After having pizza for lunch, they go back out to pick up the carpet, but there is water all over the square and the carpet seems to have floated away.

Aims

- To revise and extend prepositions for location.
- To introduce the present perfect with *ever*.

Language

New language
Have you ever had pizza?

Prepositions: in front of, next to, on the left / right, opposite

amazing, boot, canal, excellent, float, pick up, square

What you need

- Cassette / CD and player.

Before you begin

Sing the song from Unit 3.

Ask pupils what they remember about the ending of the story in Unit 3.

PUPIL'S BOOK pages 34 and 35

1 **Read and listen. Why does Alice want to go to a shop?**   20 minutes

PURPOSE To practise listening, speaking and reading.

LISTENING TO THE STORY Allow time for the pupils to look at the pictures and to try and read the story before playing the recording. This will help with their listening comprehension.

Play the recording and ask pupils to find the answer to the question *Why does Alice want to go to a shop? (Because she thinks that they can find the card in a card shop.)*

Ask pupils to share their ideas about how the children can find the carpet.

Further practice: Activity Book Exercise 1.

2 **Read the story again. Who can say these sentences?**   10 minutes

PURPOSE To help pupils look more closely at the story.

Note: *In this exercise, the pupils will simply need to understand the meaning of* Have you ever had pizza?, *from the story (for speech bubble 6). There is an active focus on this new structure in section 4B.*

Pupils work alone for this exercise and then compare answers in pairs.

Further practice: Activity Book Exercise 2.

Answer key and your notes

Answers
1 James   2 Gary   3 Alice   4 Gary   5 Alice
6 Gary

4A • Where's the carpet?

Answers

At a café: You can have a drink and a snack.
At a hotel: You can sleep / stay the night.
At a newsagent: You can buy a magazine or a newspaper.
At a post office: You can buy stamps / post a letter.
At a supermarket: You can buy food.
At a restaurant: You can have a meal.

Suggested answers

buy some stamps ... a post office
It's opposite the supermarket / on the left of the bank.
buy some fruit ... a supermarket
It's opposite the post office / on the right of the newsagent / on the left of the hotel.
have a pizza / meal ... a restaurant
It's on the right of / next to the bank / on the left of / next to the café.
have a drink ... a café
It's on the right of / next to the restaurant.

Answers

2 canal   3 amazing   4 pick up   5 best
6 wet   7 square   8 boot   9 travel   10 float
11 cross   12 boat

Possible answers

2 Alice talked about Venice.
4 They talked about pizza.
6 Alice said they needed a shop.
8 They had pizza for lunch.
10 They think the carpet floated away.

Answers

a Supermarket   b Post office   c Restaurant
d Café   e Bank   f Newsagent

Possible answers

3 next to the hotel   4 the café
5 next to the bank   6 the restaurant
7 next to the hotel   8 the newsagent
9 opposite the restaurant   10 the square

3a Find these places on the map. What can you buy or do there? Write a list. **15–20 minutes**

Pupils can work alone or in pairs for this exercise. Allow time for them to write their sentences first. Go round and help.

3b Work with a friend. You want to buy or do these things. Take it in turns to ask and give directions. **15–20 minutes**

Explain if necessary that *next to* means the same as *on the left / right of*. Ask the pupils to imagine that they are facing the bank. Ask *Where's the restaurant?* and elicit *On the right of the bank*. Clarify that when looking at the picture, the restaurant appears to be on the left, but if they were asking directions, they would be in the street.

PAIRWORK Pupils continue in pairs asking and answering based on the pictures. Go round and help.

Further practice: Activity Book Exercises 3, 4 and 5.

4 Sing a song. *Have you ever seen such a crazy thing?* **10 minutes**

See Pupil's Book page 63 for the words. Show the pupils where they can find the words before playing the recording.

See **A–Z: Songs** on page 91.

ACTIVITY BOOK pages 34 and 35

1 Circle the words. Then match the words and the meanings. **10 minutes**

Pupils circle the words and match them with the meanings.

2 Look at page 34 in your Pupil's Book. Write sentences to complete the story. **10–15 minutes**

Pupils write sentences to complete the story.

3 Read the sentences. Think. Write the places on the map. All the sentences must be true. **10–15 minutes**

Pupils read the sentences and label the map.

4 Sam is at Jack's house. Look at the map in Exercise 3 and complete Jack's message. **12 minutes**

Pupils complete the message using information from the map. Explain that there are different possible answers.

5 Write sentences about your school, your home or your town. **15 minutes**

Pupils use the phrases to write about their school, home or town.

4B • Language time

Aim
- To practise the grammar and vocabulary from section 4A.

Language
New language
Present perfect with *ever*

Past participles (irregular forms): been, broken, had, made, run, seen, written

Directions: Go straight on. Take the second road on the right. Turn left. Turn right at the bank. It's on the left.

What you need
- Cassette / CD and player.

Before you begin
Sing the song from section 4A.

PUPIL'S BOOK pages 36 and 37

1 **Listen to Amy and Max. Answer the questions.**   15 minutes

PURPOSE To introduce the present perfect with *ever* and to practise listening intensively.

Note: It usually takes a long time for pupils to understand the uses of the present perfect. In this unit, pupils meet the present perfect for the first time to ask and answer about an experience with ever. *They practise it through the interrogative and short answer forms with the 'chunk' of language* Have you ever ...? *and* Yes, I have. / No, I haven't.

Make sure the pupils understand the questions before you play the recording. Play it all through once and then again pausing it if necessary.

2a **Work with a friend. One of you is A and the other is B. Ask and answer. Have you done the same things?**   15–20 minutes

PURPOSE To practise speaking with the present perfect and *ever*.

Practise the questions and answers with the class once or twice before they start.

PAIRWORK Pupils work in pairs and take turns to ask and answer the questions truthfully.

2b **Tell the class some things you and your friend have and haven't done.**   10 minutes

PURPOSE To practise speaking with the third person singular and the first person singular and plural of the present perfect.

Pupils share the information they have learnt about each other with the class. If you have a large class, it may be better to hear a few examples and then divide the pupils into groups of four or six to continue exchanging information. Go round and help.

Answer key, tapescript and your notes

Tapescript

Amy:	What are you going to do this weekend, Max?
Max:	I'm going to the skateboard park.
Amy:	Wow! That's exciting.
Max:	Yes, it is! Have you ever been to the skateboard park?
Amy:	No! I've never been on a skateboard in my life!
Max:	What! That's terrible! You haven't been on a skateboard!
Amy:	No, Max. I do other things. I play volleyball.
Max:	Oh, volleyball.
Amy:	Well, have you ever played volleyball?
Max:	No. Never.
Amy:	What! You've never played volleyball! That's terrible!
Max:	OK, OK! Sorry!
Amy:	Volleyball is great. We play in lots of competitions.
Max:	Ah, but have you ever won a competition?
Amy:	No! But we try hard! We will win one day!
Max:	We don't have skateboarding competitions. We just do crazy tricks in the park.
Amy:	What! That's dangerous!
Max:	No, it isn't. Volleyball is more dangerous!
Amy:	No, it isn't. If you fall, you can break your leg or something. Have you ever broken anything?
Max:	No, only my skateboard!
Amy:	Oh dear!

1 Answers

1 Max has been on a skateboard / to the skateboard park but Amy hasn't.
2 Amy has played volleyball but Max hasn't.

Answers

Group 1: made been run broken seen
Group 2: lived camped cooked

Answers

2 Go straight on.   3 Turn right at the bank.
4 Take the second road on the right.

Tapescript
You're at the bank. Go straight on. Turn right. Take the second road on the left. Go straight on. Take the second road on the right. Take the first road on the left. It's on the left. Where are you now?

Answer
the café

Further practice: Activity Book Exercise 1.

3a Find the verbs in Exercise 2a. Can you see a pattern? How are the verbs in Group 2 the same? **15 minutes**

PURPOSE To focus on the form of the past participle.

Ask pupils to copy the chart into their exercise books and then to complete it with the verbs from Exercise 2a. Ask them to compare in pairs and then put the chart on the board.

Elicit the regular '-ed' pattern of the verbs in Group 2 and encourage pupils to see that the Group 1 verbs are all irregular in the past simple too.

3b Write six questions. Use three verbs from each group. **15 minutes**

PURPOSE To practise writing with the present perfect.

Pupils work alone and write six questions using three verbs from each column.

3c Work with a friend. Ask and answer. Find two things that you have both done and two things that only one of you has done. **8 minutes**

PURPOSE To develop fluency with present perfect questions.

Before dividing the class into pairs, remind the pupils that they are trying to find two things that they have both done and two things that only one of them has done.

PAIRWORK Pupils work in pairs and ask and answer using the questions they wrote in Exercise 3b. Go round and help as necessary. If they struggle to find things that they have both done or not done, you may want to give other participles that they can use, perhaps limiting it to regular verbs, for example *watched (a particular TV programme), travelled (by plane / boat)*. If you do this, encourage them to add the participles to the Group 2 list in their exercise books.

Further practice: Activity Book Exercise 2.

4a Match the directions and the pictures. **6 minutes**

PAIRWORK To introduce directions.

Do the activity orally as a whole class, checking the pronunciation of *straight*.

4b You're at the bank. Listen and follow. Where are you now? **10 minutes**

Allow time for the pupils to look closely at the map before playing the recording. If you think it may be necessary, practise giving directions that are different from the tapescript opposite, and ask the pupils to follow with their fingers. Make sure that they understand which way they are facing and therefore which is left or right.

Play the recording all through once, asking the pupils to follow with their fingers. Play it again, pausing after each direction.

4c Work with a friend. Take it in turns to give directions. **15 minutes**

PAIRWORK To develop fluency with giving directions.

Pupils work in pairs and give directions to different places on the map.

EXTRA IDEAS Fast finishers can add other places to their maps and continue giving directions.

Alternatively, pupils can draw a map of their town, label the places and write directions based on it. The maps and directions can then go into each pupil's **portfolio**.

Further practice: Activity Book Exercises 3 and 4.

ACTIVITY BOOK pages 36 and 37

1 Answer 'Yes, I have' and give more information, or 'No, I haven't'. Compare with your friends in the next lesson. **10 minutes**

Pupils complete the table. Encourage them to use a range of language when they give more information.

PAIRWORK If pupils do this for homework, allow time in the next lesson for them to ask and compare their answers in pairs.

2 Complete the questions for the answers. **8 minutes**

Pupils complete the present perfect questions for the answers given.

3 Follow the directions. Write the places. **12 minutes**

Pupils read and follow the directions. They write where they arrive.

Note: Explain if necessary that you can say Take the first on the left *or* the first road on the left *or* the first turning on the left. *It may be useful to compare these phrases with the pupils' own language.*

4 Choose two places. Write the directions. Ask your friend in the next lesson. **12 minutes**

Pupils choose two places and write directions from these places to other places on the map.

PAIRWORK If pupils do this for homework, allow time in the next lesson for them to ask and answer in pairs. This checks that what they have written makes sense, but you may need to go round and help.

Answers
2 Have you ever had pasta?
3 Have you ever seen / watched a film in English?
4 Have you ever been to Africa?

Answers
2 Brown's supermarket
3 Smith's supermarket   4 Sue's café

4C • Follow the sea!

Topic

Alice asks the others which way the sea is going. They look at the timetable of when the tide is going in and out. They work out that the sea is taking the carpet into the canal. They hire a gondola and find the carpet in the water. They put the card into the control panel and Laya appears with another code and clue. Gary touches the map and Alice is angry with him.

Aim

- To introduce digital times.

Language

New language

Oh seven forty-five.
That's quarter to eight.

bossy, difficult, everywhere, few, gondola, oar, sea, timetable

What you need

- Cassette / CD and player.

Before you begin

Sing the song from section 4A.

Answer key, tapescript and your notes

Answers

2 Alice.   3 Because he takes the oar from the man.   4 James.   5 Alice.   6 Gary.

Tapescript

Girl: *Ben, do you know how to say digital times?*
Boy: *Yes!*
Girl: *What's number one?*
Boy: *That's oh seven fifteen. And number two is twenty twenty.*
Girl: *OK, so you say the numbers in pairs. So number three is seventeen thirty-five and number four is fourteen fifty.*
Boy: *That's right! And number five is oh five forty-five.*
Girl: *And number six is oh nine thirty.*
Boy: *Yes, it's easy!*

Answers

2 = e   3 = a   4 = d   5 = f   6 = b

PUPIL'S BOOK pages 38 and 39

1 **Read and listen. What does Alice think about Gary?**   20 minutes

PURPOSE To practise listening, speaking and reading.

LISTENING TO THE STORY Allow time for pupils to look at the pictures before playing the recording. Ask pupils what they can see in each picture.

Play the recording and ask pupils to find the answer to the question *What does Alice think about Gary? (She thinks that he's very bossy.)*

Ask pupils if they can work out the code to find the next destination *(the Rocky Mountains in Canada).*

Further practice: Activity Book Exercises 1 and 2.

2 **Read the story again. Answer the questions.**   15 minutes

PURPOSE To help pupils look more closely at the story.

Pupils read the story carefully and answer the questions. They compare their answers in a small group and then share them with the class.

Further practice: Activity Book Exercise 3.

3 **Match the digital times and the clocks. Can you say the digital times in English? Listen and check.**   12 minutes

PURPOSE To practise saying digital times.

Refer back to the story and practise other times, for example *oh eight twenty-five* or *twenty-two fifteen.* Pupils then match the digital clocks with the traditional clocks below. Ask pupils to tell you when their favourite television programmes are on using digital times.

Play the recording to allow the pupils to hear the digital times and then check answers to the matching task. Look at the box with the class and check that everyone understands digital times.

4 In Venice they have water buses. Work with a friend. Look at the timetable. Take it in turns to choose a time, ask and answer.   **12 minutes**

PURPOSE To develop fluency with digital and analogue times.

Allow time for pupils to look at the times on the clocks in both columns and the timetable. They may want to write the times under the clocks in digital time before they start.

PAIRWORK Pupils take it in turns to change the time in the dialogue to one of those shown on the clocks. They can also decide whether they want to go to Lido or to the train station. The other person then checks the timetable and says when the next water bus leaves. Go round and help.

Further practice: Activity Book Exercise 4.

ACTIVITY BOOK pages 38 and 39

1 Complete the puzzle.   **12–15 minutes**

Pupils complete the puzzle.

2 Look at another message from Laya. Write what it says.   **5 minutes**

Pupils read Laya's message in the same code as in the story. They write out the message.

3 Read the text. Choose the right words and write them on the line.   **15 minutes**

Note: This activity type is in the Reading & Writing paper of the Cambridge YLE Flyers exam (see page vii). Further practice is provided in the tests.

Pupils read the summary of the story. They choose the correct words and write them in the gaps.

4 Match the times in words with the clocks. Write the missing words.   **12 minutes**

Pupils match the times with the clocks and complete the missing numbers.

Answers

It's twenty past seven.
To the train station: Oh seven fifty / ten to eight
It's half past eleven.
To Lido: Eleven forty / twenty to twelve
To the train station: Twelve fifteen / quarter past twelve
It's twenty to nine.
To Lido: Oh nine fifteen / quarter past nine
To the train station: Oh nine thirty / half past nine
It's half past two.
To Lido: Fourteen fifty / ten to three
To the train station: Fourteen fifty-five / five to three
It's three o'clock.
To Lido: Fifteen twenty / twenty past three
To the train station: Fifteen thirty-five / twenty-five to four
It's ten past five.
To Lido: Seventeen twenty / twenty past five
To the train station: Seventeen forty / twenty to six

Answers

2 Excuse me   3 timetable   4 difficult
5 screamed   6 together   7 genius
8 gondola   9 touch   10 bossy   11 fast
12 card   13 snow   14 few   15 sea   16 oar

Answer

You will need a tent in the next place.

Answers

2 an   3 to   4 went   5 of   6 wasn't   7 at
8 that   9 going   10 found   11 saw   12 it
13 on   14 put   15 Where

Answers

² twenty-five to two = c ... k = ¹² thirteen thirty-five
³ quarter past three = e ... g = ⁷ oh three fifteen
⁴ twenty past six = a ... l = ¹¹ eighteen twenty
⁵ ten to six = f ... h = ⁸ seventeen fifty
⁶ ten past eight = b ... i = ¹⁰ oh eight ten

4D • Know it all! Venice

Topic

The pupils learn about Venice, both past and present. You could have ready more information about this topic (for Pupil's Book Exercises 1 and 2), about Amsterdam (for Activity Book Exercises 1a and 1b) and about old cities in your country (for the pupils' project).

Project work

The pupils find out and write about an old city in their country.

Language

New language
bridge, festival, gondolier, historical, impossible, instead, mask, motorboat, normal, unusual, regatta, sand

What you need

- Cassette / CD and player.

English Control Panel: *Remind pupils to start completing their English Control Panels for Unit 4.*

Learning skills: *The focus in this unit is on the pupils checking their own work. You may want to allow time in class to discuss the ideas.*

Answer key, tapescript and your notes

Suggested answers

A
1 It has the shape of a fish, it doesn't have streets, cars, buses, taxis and lorries. There are many canals.
2 Sand and wood.
3 Gondolas are special boats and gondoliers are the men who control them with oars.
4 It is a boat race.
B
1 Because there are so many canals.
2 Because there was only sand.
3 Because it is a festival / *carnevale*.
4 At the regatta.

PUPIL'S BOOK pages 40 and 41

1 Venice is very unusual. Look at the pictures. What can you see there? What can't you see that there is in other cities?   **15–20 minutes**

PURPOSE To learn about Venice and to practise reading.

Discuss the pictures as a class and elicit everyone's ideas. The pupils will read the text in detail in Exercise 2.

2 Work with a friend. One of you is A and the other is B. Read your questions. Find the answers in the text in Exercise 1 and tell your friend.   **15 minutes**

PURPOSE To share knowledge and to develop fluency.

PAIRWORK Pupils focus on the questions and read the text to find the answers. They then tell each other the information they have found.

Note: *While they are reading, you may like to ask pupils to use the 'traffic light system'. As they read, they underline in pencil all the words that they already know. Then as they read in more detail, they write (or underline if they are allowed to write in their books) new words that they can guess in green, words that they can guess but are unsure about in orange and words that they don't understand in red. They first ask their partner the meaning of the words in red. Write any remaining 'red' words on the board and explain them.*

See **A–Z: Vocabulary** on page 93.

Further practice: Activity Book Exercises 1a and 1b.

3 Complete the leaflet with ideas from the text. ☐ 10 minutes

PURPOSE To practise reading and writing.

Pupils work alone and write their answers and then compare with a partner. There may be some variation in answers so at the end of the exercise collect in the ideas and put them on the board.

Further practice: Activity Book Exercise 2.

 4a Venice has a lot of problems with water. Look at the pictures and talk about these questions. ☐ 10 minutes

PURPOSE To develop fluency.

Pupils work in pairs or groups, look at the pictures very carefully and compare their ideas. It doesn't matter if their ideas are not correct at this point. Put their ideas on the board so that they can compare with the recording in the next exercise.

*Note: As this is a fluency exercise, there is no need to correct the pupils as they give their ideas but if pupils make a mistake, you can repeat the sentence correctly as you write it on the board. See **A–Z: Fluency** on page 83.*

 4b Listen to Professor Know It All. Check your answers. ☐ 12–15 minutes

Play the recording. Circle ideas on the board as the professor mentions them.

Suggested answers

2 it hasn't got any normal streets / there are many canals
3 gondolas and motorboats
4 they don't stand on the ground
5 (the) 'carnevale'
6 the regatta

Tapescript

Int = Interviewer **Prof** = Professor

Int: Hello and welcome! Once again we have our expert on everything here with us! Today Professor Know It All is going to tell us about Venice. Professor, Venice has lots of problems with water. Why is that?

Prof: Hello. Yes, well, Venice has a big problem with water! About 100 days every year, the water rises too much and it comes into the city.

Int: Why does that happen, Professor?

Prof: Well, Venice is very old. In the past it was a big, important city but now it is much bigger. There are more buildings and the canals are not very wide. The sea can't escape from the canals.

Int: Oh, I see. The sea can't escape from the canals.

Prof: Yes, the sea can't escape and so the water rises. Another reason is that Venice is lower now than it was.

Int: It's lower now?

Prof: Yes, they took too much water from the ground and the buildings dropped! Now, when the water comes in, it easily goes into the city.

Int: And what does this do to the city?

Prof: Well, it's very bad for the buildings. It destroys the walls and floors. And it's impossible to live a normal life. You can't leave things downstairs.

Int: Professor, what can they do about it?

Prof: Well, they have a plan. They want to build a special machine to stop the sea. The machine is like an electric door. When the sea rises, the door will close.

Int: That's incredible, Professor. Is it going to work?

Prof: Well, we don't know yet. We have to see what happens in the future.

Int: Well, Professor, that's very interesting. Many thanks. And that's all we have time for today. So it's goodbye from me.

Prof: And goodbye from me!

Answers

1 There are more buildings, Venice is lower than it was before, and the canals are not very wide so the sea can't escape.

2 It destroys the buildings and makes normal life very difficult. People can't leave anything downstairs in their houses.

3 They can make a machine, like a door, which closes when the sea comes in.

Your project

PURPOSE To allow pupils time to develop their own research and writing skills.

Have ready more information from encyclopaedias and websites about other interesting, old or unusual cities both in and outside the pupils' country. Ask pupils to look if they have access to the Internet. Pupils then work alone to produce a poster, a tourist leaflet or presentation about their city.

FOLLOW UP Leave time in a future lesson for posters and leaflets to be displayed in the classroom and for pupils to circulate to look at them.

See **A–Z: Project work** on page 90.

ACTIVITY BOOK pages 40 and 41

New vocabulary in Activity Book 4D: flat, houseboat, land (n), lean

Answers
2 = c 3 = a 4 = b

1a Read about another city with canals. Match the texts and the pictures. | 8–10 minutes

Pupils read the texts and match them with the pictures.

1b Answer the questions. | 20 minutes

Pupils answer the questions.

Suggested answers
2 Because the houses stand on wood in the ground and it breaks.
3 Because it is very flat.
4 Yes, because it is very flat and below the level of the sea.

2 Stefaan lives on a houseboat in Amsterdam. Complete the text. | 15 minutes

Pupils complete the text with the words in the box.

Learning skills: Writing

Answers
2 electricity 3 different 4 space 5 walk
6 hear 7 quiet 8 cold 9 make 10 cheap

Pupils can do this activity at home, but it is useful to allow time in class to discuss the idea first. You may like to expand the list of mistakes into a class list that the pupils can use when they are writing at school.

Encourage the pupils to check and correct their work at home in this way whenever they do a writing task.

See **A–Z: Errors** on page 83.

English Control Panel

Check that the pupils have completed their English Control Panel for Unit 4, whether in class or at home.

EXTRA IDEA Fast finishers can do further work on their project.

EXTRA PRACTICE There are photocopiable *Extra practice* exercises for this unit on pages 102 and 103. The answers are on pages 108 and 109.

UNIT TEST There is a photocopiable *Test* for this unit on pages 116 and 117. The tapescript and answers are on page 124.

Revision

Topic
This section contains revision exercises.

Aim
- To revise the language covered in Units 3 and 4.

Language
Revision
Future simple
First conditional
Present perfect with *ever*
New language
engine, go skiing, sail, shark

PUPIL'S BOOK pages 42 and 43

Answer key, tapescript and your notes

1a Max is going to the beach for the day. Look at his things. What do you think he will do? **15 minutes**

PURPOSE To revise the future simple.

This activity can be done orally as a class or in small groups. Alternatively pupils could work alone and write as many sentences as they can. If you wish, they can then compare their answers in small groups as a competition. The person with the most sentences which no one else has written is the winner.

1b Work with a friend. Ask and answer about the words in the box. Give a reason. **15 minutes**

PURPOSE To develop fluency with questions and answers in the future simple.

Practise the model dialogues as a whole class to demonstrate the activity.

PAIRWORK Pupils then take it in turns to ask a question with a phrase from the box for their partner to answer.

1c Can you think of more questions? **8 minutes**

Pupils can work on their own or in pairs. They think of more questions about what Max will and won't do on the beach, for example:

Will he eat an ice-cream? Will he have a picnic? Will he build a sandcastle? Will he sunbathe?

2 Imagine that you are going to the beach tomorrow. What will you do there? Write five sentences. **8 minutes**

Pupils work alone and write five sentences. Encourage stronger students to think of ideas that they have not used in the previous exercises.

Further practice: Activity Book Exercises 3a and 3b.

Possible answers
He'll go swimming.
He'll go fishing.
He'll play cards.
He'll phone his friends and family.
He'll go walking.
He'll play tennis.
He'll write in his diary.
He'll read his magazine / book.
He'll draw / paint pictures.
He'll take some photos.
He'll listen to music.

Tapescript

Suddenly the engine in Josh's boat went BANG! and stopped. He looked at the sea. It was full of sharks! 'Oh no!' he thought. 'If I jump in the water, the sharks will eat me.'* Just then, Josh saw a ship. 'I can shout!' he said. 'No, they are too far away. If I shout, they won't hear me.* I know!' he said. 'I can light a fire with my sail! No, that's not a good idea! If I light a fire with my sail, I won't be able to control the boat.'* He looked around. 'I can use my shirt!' he said. 'Hmm. No. It's getting cold. If I light a fire with my shirt, I'll be cold later.'* He looked inside the boat. 'A radio!' he said. 'Oh no! It hasn't got any batteries!' Then he saw a torch. 'Good!' he said. 'I can use the batteries from the torch! Oh no! It'll be dark soon! If I use the batteries from the torch, I won't have any light at night.'* Josh was very hungry and thirsty, but he only had one bottle of water and some cake. 'I'll be here for days!' he said. 'If I drink the water now, I'll be thirsty later.* And if I eat the cake now, I won't have any food.'* Suddenly, there was a loud voice. 'Josh!' the voice said. 'When are you coming out of the bath? If you don't come out now, I'll break the door down.'

Possible answers

1 the sharks will eat me
2 they won't hear me
3 I won't be able to control the boat
4 I'll be cold later
5 I won't have any light at night
6 I'll be thirsty later
7 I won't have any food
8 I'll break the door down

3a Read a story about Josh and his boat. Complete it with your own ideas. 12–15 minutes

PURPOSE To revise the first conditional.

Pupils complete the story with their own ideas, using the first conditional. You may like to complete the first gap as a class to model a first conditional answer. Pupils will compare their ideas with the recording in the next exercise.

3b Listen to the story. Did you have the same ideas? 12 minutes

Play the recording all through once for pupils to get the main idea and then play it through again slowly, pausing at the * given in the tapescript. However, make sure pupils understand that other ideas are valid and ask them to tell the class.

4a Work in groups. Look at the pictures. Make 'Have you ever ...?' questions to ask another group. 15 minutes

PURPOSE To revise the present perfect with *ever* and to practise speaking.

Explain the activity and read the *Think about your questions!* notes with the class.

GROUPWORK Pupils work in small groups and brainstorm interesting questions based on the pictures using *Have you ever ...?* The aim is to make as many questions that are different from other groups' questions. This encourages the pupils to use a wide vocabulary. Set a time limit and make sure that groups write their questions down.

4b Play the game. Take it in turns to ask and answer. 15 minutes

Tell the pupils to put all their pencils and pens away, as they are not allowed to add further questions at this point. Invite the groups in turn to ask another group a question. They win a point for each question they ask which no one else has. They win another point if the group they ask has to give a negative answer. If a group gives a positive answer, they must be able to answer a further question giving details. Everyone can invent answers, to encourage fluency. The group with the most points when everyone has asked all their questions are the winners.

Further practice: Activity Book Exercises 2a, 2b and 4.

ACTIVITY BOOK pages 42 and 43

1 How well can you remember your English? Put a cross ✗ on the arrow. 15 minutes

See page 30. After the pupils have put the crosses on the arrows, remind them to start with the exercise that gives them more practice in the area where they feel weakest:

describe where things are and give directions: Exercises 2a and 2b
talk about the future: Exercises 3a and 3b
say digital times: Exercise 4

2a Look at the map. Where are these places? | 15–20 minutes

Pupils use phrases of position to describe where the places are.

2b Read and complete the directions. | 12 minutes

Pupils read and complete the directions.

3a Jack wants to go to Venice. How many true sentences can you make? | 10 minutes

Pupils match the parts of the sentences to make as many true sentences as possible. Suggested answers are given opposite but the pupils may feel that more combinations are also valid.

3b What will Jack do in Venice? Complete the sentences. | 10 minutes

Pupils complete the future simple sentences.

4 Look at the train timetable. Answer the questions. | 15 minutes

Pupils look at the timetable and answer the questions using digital and analogue times.

Answers
2 The Post Office is opposite the City Centre Bank.
3 The Corner café is next to Green's supermarket.
4 Black's supermarket is on the right of the Park Hotel.

Possible answers
2 Go out of the door and turn right. Turn left and then take the first (road / turning) on the right. It's on your right.
3 Go out of the door and turn left. Go straight on. Cross the road and go straight on. Take the first (road / turning) on the right. It's on your right.
4 Go out of the door and turn right. Take the first (road / turning) on the right and then walk past the supermarket. The Corner café is on the left of the supermarket.

Answers
1 = d, e   2 = c, e   3 = c, d, e   4 = b   5 = a

Answers
2 He'll walk / go over the bridges.
3 He'll send / write a postcard to his parents.
4 He'll buy some presents for his friends.
5 He'll eat a pizza.
6 He'll see a gondola. /
He'll ride / go / travel in a gondola.
7 He'll see the canals.
8 He'll stay in an old hotel.

Answers
2 It's at fifteen thirty. That's half past three.
3 It's at sixteen forty. That's twenty to five.
4 It's at eighteen oh five. That's five past six.

5A • Bears!

Topic

Gary, Alice and James fly on the carpet and stop to buy food, a tent and a torch for their time in the Rocky Mountains. Alice tells the others about the brown bears in the mountains. They arrive at a campsite and decide to look for the control card in the morning, so they put up the tent and go to sleep. In the middle of the night, they hear a noise and can see something pushing on the tent from outside.

Aims

- To introduce the present perfect with *just*.
- To revise the zero conditional.

Language

Revision
If you want to walk, talk loudly and sing.
New language
I've just read this paper.

Past simple (irregular forms): ate, brought, heard, woke up

Past participle (irregular form): read

aloud, biscuit, campsite, cloud, ground, hang, noise, outside, path, put up, reply, still, wake up, whisper

What you need

- Cassette / CD and player.

Before you begin

Sing the song from Unit 4.

Ask pupils what they remember about the ending of the story in Unit 4.

Answer key and your notes

Answers

2 True. They are going to stay in the Rocky Mountains.

3 True. He asks, 'How did you do that?'

4 True. The paper says that you must be very careful.

5 False. They can hear a noise and see something pushing on the tent.

6 False. They decided to look for it in the morning.

7 False. Alice woke up first.

8 True. He had biscuits in the tent.

PUPIL'S BOOK pages 44 and 45

1 **Read and listen. Why does Gary think that the bears are outside?** 20 minutes

PURPOSE To practise listening, speaking and reading.

LISTENING TO THE STORY Allow time for the pupils to look at the pictures and to try and read the story before playing the recording. This will help with their listening comprehension.

Play the recording and ask pupils to find the answer to the question *Why does Gary think that the bears are outside? (Because something is pushing on the tent and because James had biscuits in the tent.)*

Ask pupils to share their ideas of what Gary, Alice and James can do.

Further practice: Activity Book Exercise 1.

2 **Read the story again. Write 'True', 'False' or 'We don't know'. Give a reason.** 10 minutes

PURPOSE To help pupils look more closely at the story.

Pupils work alone for this exercise and then compare answers with a partner.

Further practice: Activity Book Exercises 2 and 3.

3a Bears are dangerous! What should you do in the Rockies? Tell the class your ideas. — 8 minutes

PURPOSE To develop fluency.

Encourage the pupils to use the pictures for ideas. To generate more language, try not to focus on the phrases in Exercise 3b.

Note: The Rocky Mountains are often known simply as 'the Rockies'.

3b Find two pieces of advice for each topic. — 10 minutes

PURPOSE To revise the zero conditional.

Pupils can work alone or in pairs to match the advice from the box with the bear safety topics in the leaflet.

3c What other ideas did you have in Exercise 3a? — 5 minutes

Pupils share their additional ideas with the class.

EXTRA IDEA Ask pupils to think of another sport or activity and to write similar sentences giving advice. This can then go into each child's **portfolio**.

Further practice: Activity Book Exercise 4.

4 🔊 Sing a song. *Please don't tell me about the big grizzly bear!* — 10 minutes

See Pupil's Book page 63 for the words. Show the pupils where they can find the words before playing the recording.

See **A–Z: Songs** on page 91.

ACTIVITY BOOK pages 44 and 45

1 Circle the words. Then match the words and the meanings. — 8 minutes

Pupils circle the words and match them with the meanings.

2 Complete the sentences. Which story? Match the sentences and the pictures. — 12 minutes

Pupils complete the sentences with the verbs of speech from the box and then match them with the picture from the correct story. Make sure they understand that the pictures do not match the text exactly, but that they have to identify the story from the picture.

3 Look at page 44 in your Pupil's Book. Answer the questions. — 12 minutes

Pupils read the story and answer the questions.

4 Read about camping. Match the advice and the reasons. Write the missing reasons. — 15 minutes

Pupils match the advice with the reasons and write the missing reasons.

Answers

If you want to walk,
... don't go off the path.
... talk loudly or sing.
If you want to camp,
... don't camp near bear tracks.
... only camp in campsites.
If you have food,
... don't put it in your tent.
... hang it in plastic bags in a tree.
If you want to cook,
... do it 100 metres from your tent.
... put your cooking clothes in a bag in a tree.
If you see a bear,
... don't move suddenly.
... stand still, and wait for the bear to move away.

Answers

2 land   3 biscuit   4 tent   5 torch   6 cloud
7 ground   8 sleep   9 whisper   10 eat
11 wake up   12 smile

Answers

2 screamed = a   5 replied = f
3 asked = d   6 whispered = e
4 shouted = c

Answers

2 In the Rocky Mountains.
3 Food, a (big) tent and a torch.
4 Alice.
5 Do not put food in your tent.
6 They ate the food from the shop.
7 Because it was cold outside. / To sleep.
8 A noise.
9 With the torch.
10 Something was pushing on the tent.

Suggested answers

2 = j The sun can burn you.
3 = h   4 = a   5 = i   6 = b   7 = e
8 = k Animals can get in.
9 = g
10 = l Fires are very dangerous.
11 = f   12 = c

5B • Language time

Aim
- To practise the grammar and vocabulary from section 5A.

Language
Revision
Future simple
New language
Present perfect with *just*
Past simple (irregular form): left
Past participles (irregular forms): bought, fallen, found, put, taken, woken up
back, can (n), forward, rubbish

What you need
- Cassette / CD and player.
- Dice and counters for each group of four (for Pupil's Book Exercise 3).

Before you begin
Sing the song from section 5A.

Answer key, tapescript and your notes

Tapescript

Amy: Hi, Max. What are you doing?
Max: Walking slowly! I've just fallen off my skateboard!*
Amy: I told you it was dangerous!
Max: No, it's not. I always use pads and I've just got a new helmet.* Oh, it'll be OK.
Amy: I hope so!
Max: What are **you** doing?
Amy: I've just finished a volleyball game. We've just won the competition!*
Max: Wow! That's great!
Amy: Yes! We've just played five teams and we won the cup!
Max: Excellent. Are you going home now?
Amy: Yes! I have to take this certificate home. They've just given it to me.*
Max: Oh OK.
Amy: And Mum's just telephoned.* She's waiting outside the park for me. She and Dad have just been to the supermarket* so we have to take the shopping home.
Max: OK, Amy. I'll see you later.
Amy: Bye!
Max: Bye!

Answers

1 He's just fallen off his skateboard.
2 She's just won a volleyball competition.

PUPIL'S BOOK pages 46 and 47

1a Listen to Amy and Max. Answer the questions. — 15 minutes

PURPOSE To introduce the present perfect with *just*.

Allow pupils time to read the questions. Then play the recording all through once for general meaning and then again for pupils to listen carefully to the answers. Pupils write down the answers while they are listening.

1b Listen again. Make a sentence with 'just' about each of these things. — 10 minutes

PURPOSE To practise listening intensively and to practise speaking with the present perfect and *just*.

Before playing the recording again, allow time for pupils to look at the pictures and to try and remember what Amy and Max said. Then play the recording again, pausing at the * given in the tapescript to allow time for the pupils to write their answers.

After checking answers, ask pupils how they can say these sentences in their own language. If they don't understand, explain that we use the present perfect with *just* for something that happened not long ago. Ask the pupils to give you some examples from their own experience.

If pupils need further practice, invite volunteers to open the door / window / a book, to put a book on your desk, to write something on the board, etc. Elicit sentences with the present perfect and *just* using the participles covered so far.

Further practice: Activity Book Exercise 2.

2a Work with a friend. What have the people just done? Take it in turns to say a sentence and guess. **12 minutes**

PURPOSE To practise the present perfect with *just*.

PAIRWORK Pupils work in pairs taking it in turns to say a sentence, using an idea from the box, for their partner to identify the person or people in the picture. Go round and help.

Further practice: Activity Book Exercise 3.

2b Think. Write the names. **10 minutes**

PURPOSE To practise the present perfect negative with *just*.

You can do this as a written activity or orally in pairs, with the pupils taking it in turns to say the sentence or the name(s).

3 Play the game. Remember the rules for the Rocky Mountains! **15–20 minutes**

PURPOSE To develop fluency with the present perfect and the future simple.

Ask the pupils to look back at the advice on page 45. Then discuss the game before you divide the class into small groups.

GROUPWORK Give out dice and counters to each group. To start, they roll the dice and the person with the highest number starts. They then roll again in turn and move their counters to the correct square. On a green square, they say what they have just done and on a blue square they say what they will do. On other squares, they follow the instructions. If they make a mistake, they miss a turn. The person who finishes first is the winner.

Further practice: Activity Book Exercise 1.

ACTIVITY BOOK pages 46 and 47

1 Imagine that you are going camping. Look at Exercise 4 on page 45. Write what you will and won't do. **15 minutes**

Pupils look back at Exercise 4 on page 45. They then read the sentences and write future simple sentences about what they will and won't do on a camping trip.

2 Max isn't very happy. He's talking to Amy. Write the numbers in the boxes to complete the conversation. **12 minutes**

Pupils choose the correct sentence for each gap and write the number in the box.

3 What has just happened to these people? Look at the pictures and find the differences. **15–20 minutes**

Pupils write sentences as in the example to describe what has happened.

1b Answers
2 Max has just got a new helmet.
3 Amy's team has just won the volleyball cup.
4 They have just given her the certificate.
5 Amy's mum has just telephoned her.
6 Amy's mum and dad have just been to the supermarket.

Answers
2 Cath 3 Tina 4 Jorge 5 Dan
6 Wen and Lu

Suggested answers
2 I'll take / use sun cream. / I'll wear a hat.
3 I won't put up my tent under a tree / on a hill.
4 I won't drink river water. / I'll drink bottled water.
5 I'll be careful with the fire.
6 I'll take it / my rubbish home.

Answers
b = 6   c = 4   d = 7   e = 5   f = 2   g = 1
h = 8

Answers
In Picture A, Jackie has just had a pizza.
In Picture B, she has just walked into a man.
In Picture A, Robert has just been swimming. In Picture B, he has just bought a pizza.
In Picture A, Helen has just taken a photo. In Picture B, she has just seen a film / been to the cinema.
In Picture A, Henry has just opened the car door. In Picture B, he has just put something / a box in the car.
In Picture A, Sue has just bought a newspaper. In Picture B, she has just put the / her / newspaper in a bin.
In Picture A, Tom and Bill have just played football. In Picture B, they have just run / finished a race.
In Picture A, Pat and Keith have just had a picnic. In Picture B, they have just woken up.

5C • Don't talk!

Topic

The children sit in the dark in the tent for a long time. When they wake up in the morning, they see snow on the ground and they realise that it was snow moving on the tent, not bears pushing it. Suddenly, they see a squirrel with the control code. Alice gets the card, the next code appears and Laya gives them the next clue. Gary cracks the code and they fly off to the next destination.

Aim

- To revise past tenses and the present perfect.

Language

Revision
Something was pushing both sides of the tent.

They sat in the dark for a long time.

Yes, but they didn't come.

I've just looked outside.

New language
Past simple (irregular forms): sat, spoke

ability, safe, shine, side, size, squirrel, turn off

What you need

- Cassette / CD and player.

Before you begin

Sing the song from section 5A.

Answer key, tapescript and your notes

Answers

1 = e 2 = c 3 = b 4 = f 5 = j 6 = d
7 = g 8 = i 9 = h 10 = a

PUPIL'S BOOK pages 48 and 49

1 **Read and listen. Why does James laugh?**   20 minutes

PURPOSE To practise listening, speaking and reading.

LISTENING TO THE STORY Allow time for pupils to look at the pictures before playing the recording. Ask pupils what they can see in each picture.

Play the recording and ask pupils to find the answer to the question *Why does James laugh? (Because there weren't any bears.)*

Ask pupils if they can work out the code to find the next destination *(Brasilia)*.

Further practice: Activity Book Exercise 1.

2 **What happened in 5A and 5C? Put the sentences in the correct order.**   12 minutes

PURPOSE To help pupils look more closely at the story.

Pupils can work alone or with a partner to put the sentences in the correct order. Go round and help. Check as a whole class.

Further practice: Activity Book Exercises 2 and 3.

3a **What do you know about brown bears? Tell the class your ideas.**   10 minutes

PURPOSE To share information and to develop fluency.

Pupils look at the pictures and think about the questions. They can first work in pairs or small groups to share their information and ideas and then tell the rest of the class what they have discussed.

It doesn't matter if they are unsure about some of the questions as they will hear the answers in the next exercise.

To help with the following listening activity, you may want to ask pupils to copy the table for Exercise 3b into their exercise books and to write in the information they have collected. If they use a pencil, they can check and correct this as necessary.

3b **Listen and check your answers. Complete the table.**   12 minutes

PURPOSE To practise listening intensively.

Pupils copy the table if they have not already done so. Then play the recording all through once for general meaning. Play it again pausing at the * given in the tapescript for pupils to check and correct the information in their table.

Go through the answers as a class, accepting other valid ideas that the pupils had written in from their discussions in Exercise 3a (for example, specific things that bears eat).

Tapescript

Welcome to the Nature Programme. Today our special topic is brown bears. Brown bears live in North America, Asia and Europe. There aren't any bears at all in Africa, Australia and Antarctica.* Brown bears eat anything! They eat wild animals and fish. They also eat fruit, leaves and grass.* The biggest brown bears can be over two and a half metres tall when they stand up. They've got big, heavy bodies, large heads and small eyes.* They can do lots of things. They can run fast – up to 40 km an hour. That's as fast as a car in a town! They can swim and climb trees. They can smell very well – that's why they stand up, to smell the air – but they can't see very well.* In the summer, brown bears usually eat a lot because there isn't much food in the winter. In the winter, they sleep a lot.* Brown bears have got a lot of problems. People kill them for sport and they also destroy the places where they live. Because of this, brown bears are in danger and people are now trying to help the bears. They stop people from hunting and control the forests.

Further practice: Activity Book Exercise 4.

ACTIVITY BOOK pages 48 and 49

1 Which word is different? Give a reason.   15 minutes

Pupils write which word is different in each group and why.

2 There weren't any bears, so what happened? Write the missing sentences.   15+ minutes

Pupils write a sentence for each picture to describe what happened.

3 James is telling his friends about what happened. Correct the information.   12–15 minutes

Pupils write sentences correcting six more mistakes as in the example.

4 Read about ground squirrels. Label the pictures.   12 minutes

Pupils read the fact card and label the pictures.

Answers
Places: North America, Asia and Europe
Food: wild animals, fish, fruit, leaves, grass
Size: biggest over 2.5 metres tall
Abilities: can run fast, swim, climb trees, smell very well
Life in the summer: eat a lot
Life in the winter: sleep a lot
Problems: people kill them and destroy the places where they live

Suggested answers
3 outside – the others are colours.
4 city – the others are adjectives / describing words.
5 push – the others are names of things.
6 old – the others are things we do with our voice / verbs.
7 torch – the others are animals.
8 shine – the others are things we do with our eyes.
9 say – the others are past tense.
10 Laya – the others are real people / travelling on the carpet / children.

Suggested answers
2 It started to snow
4 There was a lot of snow on the tent.
6 In the morning, they saw that it was snow, not bears.

Answers
No! Something was pushing the tent.
No! We went to sleep.
No! I went outside the tent first.
No! There was a squirrel. / There weren't any bears.
No! The squirrel had the control card.
No! Alice got the control card.

Answers
1 28   2 eyes   3 white circle   4 20
7 bags to carry food   8 stripes
9 short legs   10 8   11 5   12 bed of grass

5D • Know it all! The Rocky Mountains

Topic

The pupils learn about the Rocky Mountains and about how people live, work and spend leisure time there. They also learn about the dinosaurs that inhabited the area. You could have ready more information about these topics (for Pupil's Book Exercises 1b and 2a and Activity Book Exercise 1) and about important places for wild animals (for the pupils' project).

Project work

The pupils find out and write about a place where there are a lot of wild animals.

Language

New language
across, canoeing, footprint, gold, landscape, mine, potato, silver, skiing, sugar, vegetable

What you need

- Cassette / CD and player.

English Control Panel: *Remind pupils to start completing their English Control Panels for Unit 5.*

Learning skills: *The focus here is on reading. You may like to look ahead and allow time in class for the pupils to discuss the idea first and then try it out as they work on the reading texts earlier in the unit.*

Answer key, tapescript and your notes

Answers
1 = a, e   2 = c, f   3 = b, d

Answers
These answers can be found in the texts:
1 In Canada and the USA.
2 Sugar, potatoes and other vegetables.
5 They go in opposite directions.
7 Gold, silver (and other metals).
8 People go camping, canoeing, walking and skiing.

Tapescript
Int = *Interviewer*   **Prof** = *Professor*

Int: *Hello! Welcome. Today we have our expert of experts, Professor Know It All, with us again. He's the man who knows everything! Professor, what can you tell us about the Rocky Mountains?*
Prof: *Well, what do you want to know?*
Int: *Well, for example, are they the same as Mount Kenya? Are they old volcanoes?*
Prof: *Oh no. The Rocky Mountains appeared when areas of land under the sea crashed into each other. This pushed the mountains up.*
Int: *Oh, I see. You mean two areas of land hit each other, and this made the mountains.*
Prof: *Yes, that's right.*
Int: *And when did that happen?*

PUPIL'S BOOK pages 50 and 51

1a Read about the Rocky Mountains. Match two pictures with each text. **10 minutes**

PURPOSE To practise skimming.

Pupils work alone. Ask them to look at the pictures and to tell you what they can see. Then ask them to read the texts as quickly as possible and to match two pictures with each text. Tell them to stop reading the text when they have found the pictures which match it. This activity will help them gain confidence in being able to skim quickly without understanding every word.

Ask pupils to identify the words that helped them match the texts and the pictures.

1b Which of these questions can you answer from the texts? Do you know the answers to the other questions? **10 minutes**

PURPOSE To practise reading and speaking.

Pupils work alone to see which questions can be answered from the texts, or which answers they already know, and make notes. They then compare with a partner. They will hear all the answers in the following exercise.

1c 📻 Listen to Professor Know It All. Check your answers. **12 minutes**

PURPOSE To practise listening for detail.

Play the recording so that pupils can check their answers to all the questions.

Further practice: Activity Book Exercise 1.

2a Millions of years ago, dinosaurs lived where the Rockies are now. Look at the pictures. Tell the class what you know about dinosaurs.

10 minutes

PURPOSE To develop fluency.

The pupils share information in groups before telling the class.

2b Listen to Professor Know It All again. Choose the correct words.

8 minutes

PURPOSE To practise listening intensively.

Allow time first for pupils to read the text. Then play the recording for them to choose the correct options. Play it through again, stopping as necessary.

Tapescript

Int: Can you tell us something more about them?

Prof: Yes, of course, well there are lots of fossils of dinosaur footprints in the Rocky Mountains. They are very big and very clear.

Int: How big are they?

Prof: Well, some of the prints are small – about ten centimetres across – but others are forty or more centimetres across. They really are amazing.

Int: How many are there?

Prof: Oh, there are lots of them! Over three hundred. Big ones and small ones.

Int: And what can we learn from the footprints?

Prof: A lot. For example, we can see how many dinosaurs there were together. We can see that there were probably about seventy-eight dinosaurs. So this tells us that they moved in big groups.

Int: Wow! That's really interesting.

Prof: Yes, and we can also see that they moved around in a family. We can see the footprints of baby dinosaurs next to the prints of older dinosaurs, probably their mothers.

Int: And can we see how big they were?

Prof: Yes, probably. If we know the size of their feet, we can say how big they were. Probably they were about nine metres long.

Int: That's big.

Prof: Yes, and if we look carefully at the print, we can see how fast they were walking.

Int: Well, most dinosaurs moved very slowly, didn't they?

Prof: Oh no! We can see from the footprints that they could move very fast.

Int: Well, thank you, Professor. That's very interesting. I hope that I can go and see the dinosaur footprints one day!

Prof: Yes, you must!

Int: So it's goodbye from me.

Prof: And goodbye from me!

Further practice: Activity Book Exercises 2a and 2b.

Your project

PURPOSE To allow pupils time to develop their own research and writing skills.

Have ready more information about other places where there are a lot of wild animals – perhaps a safari park in Africa or somewhere in your country. Pupils research the animals which lived there many years ago and why they disappeared and the animals which live there now. They could look at what they eat and the dangers to them. They then produce a poster, a booklet or a PowerPoint presentation.

1c Tapescript

Prof: Probably about seventy-five to a hundred million years ago.

Int: Oh! A long time ago! That's when the dinosaurs were living, isn't it?

Prof: Yes, that's right. In fact, you can see lots of fossils in the rocks. There are fossils of sea animals, plants and huge dinosaur footprints.

Int: Really? Dinosaur footprints! Can you tell us something more about them?

1c Answers

These answers are heard in the interview:

3 Sea animals, plants and dinosaur footprints.

4 75–100 million years old.

6 Two areas of land under the sea crashed into each other and pushed up to make the mountains.

Answers

2 40   3 300   4 big   5 next to   6 size
7 9   8 fast

FOLLOW UP Leave time in a future lesson for posters and booklets to be displayed in the classroom and for pupils to circulate to look at them. The booklets, or photos if the pupils have made a poster, can be included in each child's **portfolio**.

See **A–Z: Project work** on page 90.

ACTIVITY BOOK pages 50 and 51

New vocabulary in Activity Book 5D: captain, distance, pilot, raft

1 Read about sports activities in the Rocky Mountains. Find words for these meanings.   20 minutes

Pupils read the text and find words for the meanings.

2a Safety is very important. How many pictures can you match with each sport?   12 minutes

Pupils match the sports with as many pictures as possible. They may have different ideas if they are very involved with a particular sport.

2b Match the advice and the reasons.   10 minutes

Pupils match the advice with the reasons.

Learning skills: Reading

Pupils can do this activity at home, but it is useful to allow time in class to discuss the idea first.

Encourage the pupils to try the activity at home. When they read in class, remind them to use different strategies to work out the meaning of words.

English Control Panel

Check that the pupils have completed their English Control Panel for Unit 5, whether in class or at home.

EXTRA IDEA Fast finishers can do further work on their project.

EXTRA PRACTICE There are photocopiable *Extra practice* exercises for this unit on pages 104 and 105. The answers are on page 109.

UNIT TEST There is a photocopiable *Test* for this unit on pages 118 and 119. The tapescript and answers are on pages 124 and 125.

Answers
2 noise 3 raft 4 scary 5 captain 6 oar
7 favourite 8 pilot 9 lean 10 rapids

Suggested answers
biking: pads, a helmet, lights
paragliding: a helmet
sailing: a life jacket
skateboarding: pads, a helmet
snowboarding: goggles, special clothes
white water rafting: a life jacket

Answers
2 = f 3 = a 4 = b 5 = d 6 = e

6 Laya's final message

6A • Where is it?

Topic
Gary, Alice and James arrive in Brasilia and see the plane shape of the city. They fly towards the government buildings and land on a high bridge between two towers with water all around them. Gary finally sees the card under the bridge but they don't know how they can reach it.

Aim
- To introduce *feel / look / smell / sound / taste like*.

Language
New language
It looks like a plane.

building, cockpit, crown, finally, government, nearly, pilot, shape, towards, tower, windy, wing

What you need
- Cassette / CD and player.

Before you begin
Sing the song from Unit 5.

Ask pupils what they remember about the ending of the story in Unit 5.

PUPIL'S BOOK pages 52 and 53

1 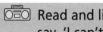 Read and listen. Why does James say, 'I can't look'?   20 minutes

PURPOSE To practise listening, speaking and reading.

LISTENING TO THE STORY Allow time for the pupils to look at the pictures and to try and read the story before playing the recording. This will help with their listening comprehension.

Play the recording and ask pupils to find the answer to the question *Why does James say, 'I can't look'? (Because he hates high places.)*

Ask pupils to share their ideas about how they can get the card.

Further practice: Activity Book Exercise 1.

2 Read the story again. Answer the questions.   10 minutes

PURPOSE To help the pupils look more closely at the story.

Pupils work alone for this exercise and then compare answers with a partner.

Further practice: Activity Book Exercise 2.

Answer key and your notes

Answers
2 James.
3 On a bridge between two towers / the government building.
4 When he's in a high place.
5 Because they were flying high on the carpet.
6 He looked under the bridge.

Suggested answers

1 two people   2 a letter 'C'
3 a snake / a sea monster   4 a pyramid
5 a letter 'H' / two books
6 a crown / a strange fruit   7 a bowl

3 Look at the pictures of Brasilia. What do the buildings look like? Tell the class your ideas or use the words in the box.   **12 minutes**

PURPOSE To introduce *look(s) like.*

Pupils look carefully at the pictures. Remind them that they should make sentences using *looks like* as in the model. They can make their own comparisons in addition to the suggested answers opposite.

Note: *See Exercise 3 on Activity Book page 53 for more information about pictures 3 and 5. The other pictures show:*
1 the Dois Candangos Monument
2 the Juscelino Kubitschek Memorial
4 the Temple of Good Will (Legião da Boa Vontade)
6 the Cathedral (Nossa Senhora Aparecida)
7 the Chamber of Deputies (Congress buildings)

Further practice: Activity Book Exercises 3 and 4.

4 🔊 Sing a song. *My friend said to me ...*   **10 minutes**

See Pupil's Book page 63 for the words. Show the pupils where they can find the words before playing the recording.

See **A–Z: Songs** on page 91.

ACTIVITY BOOK pages 52 and 53

1 Complete the words in the puzzles. Two letters are the same in each puzzle.   **12 minutes**

Pupils complete the puzzles.

Answers

2 a wings   b windy
3 a towards   b towers
4 a strange   b building
5 a nearly   b plane
6 a Brazil   b pilot
7 a bridge   b decide
8 a government   b pointing

2 Look at page 52 in your Pupil's Book. Write the name of the person or thing.   **10–15 minutes**

Pupils read the story again and write the names.

Answers

2 James   3 the church   4 the towers
5 Gary   6 Alice   7 a piece of metal
8 water

3 Seven of these sentences are about the J K bridge in Brasilia and seven are about the government buildings. Write 'B' or 'G'. Then put them in the correct order.   **15 minutes**

Pupils read and label the sentences. They then read carefully to write the sentence numbers in the correct order.

Answers

The JK bridge: 1, 10, 6, 14, 3, 5, 12
The government buildings: 8, 7, 9, 4, 2, 11, 13

4 Draw or find a picture of an unusual building that you know. Write about it.   **20 minutes**

Pupils use the space on the left to draw or stick in a picture of an unusual building. They then write about it, answering the suggested questions. Encourage the pupils to use their list of errors from Activity Book section 4D to correct their work.

EXTRA IDEA This piece of work could also be done on a separate piece of paper to go into each pupil's **portfolio**.

6B • Language time

Aim

- To practise the grammar and vocabulary from section 6A.

Language

Revision
Past tenses
First conditional
New language
feel / look / smell / sound / taste like
Past simple (irregular forms): got, had, slept
almost, blow, coffee, face, knock, next

What you need

- Cassette / CD and player.

Before you begin

Sing the song from section 6A.

PUPIL'S BOOK pages 54 and 55

Answer key, tapescript and your notes

1a Complete the sentences. Match them with the pictures. — 10 minutes

PURPOSE To practise *feel(s) / look(s) / smell(s) / sound(s) / taste(s) like.*

Pupils can work alone or in pairs. They complete the sentences and then match them with the pictures.

Answers
2 tastes = c   3 feels = d   4 sounds = b
5 smells = a

1b 🔊 Listen to the sounds. Make sentences. — 10 minutes

Allow time for pupils to look at the pictures before playing the recording. Check the vocabulary for each picture. Play the recording and pause after each sound for pupils to give their answers.

Further practice: Activity Book Exercise 1.

Tapescript
[Sound effects of:]
1 *[monkeys chattering]*
2 *[a door being opened]*
3 *[a frog croaking]*
4 *[rain]*
5 *[wind]*
6 *[a whale singing]*

2a Read the start of the story. Then put the other sentences in the correct order. Choose a sentence from A and then B. — 15 minutes

PURPOSE To practise reading.

Read the start of the story with the class. Then invite volunteers to read the sentences marked 1 and 2 from A and B respectively. Use these two sentences to explain the activity. Make sure pupils understand that they don't have to complete the sentences yet.

Check answers quickly by asking two pupils to read out the numbers in each column, A and then B.

Suggested answers
Number 1 sounds like monkeys. = c
Number 2 sounds like a door. = f
Number 3 sounds like a frog. = e
Number 4 sounds like rain. = b
Number 5 sounds like the wind. = d
Number 6 sounds like a whale. = a

Answers
The numbers should read down:
A: 5, 3, 1, 7, 11, 9
B: 4, 12, 6, 10, 8, 2

Answers

First, they ^c **went** to the Grand Canyon. Alice ⁿ **climbed** into a hole where there were snakes. Next, they ^b **were** lost in the mist in China. A boy ^g **helped** them and they ^h **slept** in a cave. After that they almost ^a **lost** the carpet on Mount Kenya. Alice ⁱ **found** a rope and ^j **got** the carpet back. Next, the carpet ^d **took** them to Venice. The sea almost ^m **carried** the carpet away. The next place they ^f **travelled** to was the Rocky Mountains. They ^k **thought** they ^l **heard** bears in the night. Next, they ^e **flew** to Brasilia and that is where they are now. James is frightened because they are up high.

Suggested answers

1 Alice wasn't sitting in the hole.

Gary wasn't wearing a hat.

2 The boy wasn't riding his donkey in China.

Alice wasn't sleeping.

The boy had a lantern.

3 The carpet wasn't on a tree on Mount Kenya.

Gary wasn't eating a sandwich.

4 Alice wasn't fishing in Venice.

Gary wasn't swimming.

James wasn't reading.

5 It wasn't snowing in the morning in the Rocky Mountains.

There wasn't a bear on the carpet.

The children weren't hiding behind a tree.

Answers

2 = g 3 = d 4 = f 5 = c 6 = b 7 = a

Answers

2 look / feel like ... paragliding

3 taste like ... orange juice

4 sound like ... bear 5 look like ... snake

6 feel like ... snow

7 taste like ... chocolate

8 sound like ... bird

Answers

2 wanted 3 discovered 4 climbed 5 saw

6 thought 7 got 8 took 9 arrived

10 found 11 came 12 slept 13 heard

14 decided 15 went

2b **Write the story in the correct order. Complete the sentences with the correct form of the verb.** 20 minutes

PURPOSE To revise past tenses.

Pupils work on their own to write the story in the correct order and to complete the sentences. You may want to refer them to their groups of regular and irregular past simple forms in their exercise books.

EXTRA IDEA Pupils can write out the story in the correct order and illustrate some or all of the events. To do this, they will need to change the verbs at the end into the past and then complete the story later with a summary of the episode in 6C. The illustrated stories can then go into each pupil's **portfolio**.

Further practice: Activity Book Exercise 2.

3 **Think about the story. What's wrong with these pictures?** 10 minutes

PURPOSE To revise past tenses.

Allow time for pupils to look at the pictures either alone or in pairs and then to write some sentences about each picture. Go round and help. Pupils may use different past tenses and have different ideas which are also valid.

Further practice: Activity Book Exercises 3, 4 and 5.

4 **The children are now in Brasilia. What can they do? Match the parts of the sentences.** 8 minutes

PURPOSE To revise the first conditional.

Allow pupils time to read the two parts of the sentence and then in pairs to take turns in saying complete sentences to each other.

ACTIVITY BOOK pages 54 and 55

1 **Complete the questions and the answers.** 15 minutes

Pupils complete the questions and answers.

2 **Do you remember Fred's terrible holiday? Complete the letter.** 12 minutes

Pupils complete Fred's letter of complaint to the hotel with the correct verb forms.

3 Look at page 52 in your Pupil's Book. Make true sentences.

12 minutes

Pupils draw lines to make as many true sentences as possible.

4 What did the children do before they landed in Brazil? Correct the sentences.

12 minutes

Pupils correct the sentences about the previous stories.

5 Max had a bad day in Unit 5. What was Amy doing when she telephoned him? Look at the picture. Write four sentences.

12–15 minutes

Pupils write four sentences based on the picture.

Answers

They have / James / Gary / Alice has just landed on the bridge.
They have / James / Gary / Alice has just flown to Brasilia.
James has just said that he feels ill.
Gary has just found the card.
Gary has just looked under the bridge.
Alice has just told them about the shape of Brasilia.

Answers

2 No! They didn't fly to France. They flew to Canada / the Rocky Mountains.
3 No! They didn't see any bears in the Rocky Mountains. They saw a squirrel.
4 No! They didn't find the card in a house. They found it in the Great Wall.
5 No! They didn't sleep in a hotel there. They slept in a cave.
6 No! They didn't go on a plane. They went on a gondola.
7 No! They didn't land on the savannah. They landed on the mountain / Mount Kenya.
8 No! James didn't throw a rope. He threw stones.

Suggested answers

She was sitting on a chair.
She was drawing.
She was eating a sandwich.
She was drinking orange juice.

6C • Goodbye!

Topic

Gary takes one of James' shoes and ties it to some string from the carpet. He throws it down at the control card, which falls into the shoe. When they put the card into the control panel, Laya appears and tells them that they can go home. They arrive back in the attic and Alice says that they must tell their parents about the adventures. Gary reveals that he is from Laya's planet. He pushes a button on the control panel and changes the carpet into a spaceship. He then disappears.

Aim

• To introduce relative clauses.

Language

New language

He grabbed one of the shoes that James was wearing!

Past simple (irregular form): knew

change, last, return, string, tie

What you need

• Cassette / CD and player.

Before you begin

Sing the song from section 6A.

Answer key, tapescript and your notes

Answers

2 James 3 Laya 4 James 5 Gary 6 Gary
7 people from Planet Zoon / Gary's people
8 Planet Zoon

Answers

2 This is the shoe that Gary used to get the control card.
3 Alice is the girl who knows a lot about things.
4 This is the button that Gary used to return to his planet / Planet Zoon.
5 James is the boy who is afraid of high places.
6 This is the carpet that changed into a spaceship.

PUPIL'S BOOK pages 56 and 57

1 🔊 **Read and listen. Where is Gary going?** `20 minutes`

PURPOSE To practise listening, speaking and reading.

LISTENING TO THE STORY Allow time for pupils to look at the pictures before playing the recording. Ask pupils what they can see in each picture.

Play the recording and ask pupils to find the answer to the question *Where is Gary going? (Home to his planet.)*

Further practice: Activity Book Exercise 1.

2 **Read the story again. Say the names.** `10 minutes`

PURPOSE To help pupils look more closely at the story.

Pupils read the sentences carefully. They compare their answers in a small group and then share them with the class.

Further practice: Activity Book Exercise 2.

3 **This information is wrong! Correct the sentences.** `10 minutes`

PURPOSE To introduce relative clauses with *who* and *that*.

Before asking pupils to correct the sentences, ask them to read them carefully and to try and work out why some sentences use *who* and some sentences use *that*. They may be able to see that we use *who* for people and *that* for things.

4 What can you see in the pictures? Make sentences. **8 minutes**

PURPOSE To revise the stories in the previous units and to introduce the relative pronoun *where*.

Use the model answer to introduce the relative pronoun *where* and explain that we use this for a place.

Pupils look at the pictures and write sentences with relative clauses using the phrases in the box. Go over the activity as a whole class.

Further practice: Activity Book Exercises 3 and 4.

5a Work in pairs. Some pairs are James and Alice and other pairs are their parents. Get ready to meet each other. **10 minutes**

Divide the class in half. One half works in pairs as James and Alice and the other half works in pairs as their parents. In each half give each pair a number.

PAIRWORK Pupils then work in their pairs and practise what they are going to say. The 'James and Alice' pairs look back at the stories to remind themselves of what they can describe to their parents and make some notes. The 'parents' look back at the stories and think of some questions to ask. They can write them down. Go round and help.

5b James and Alice have just run to see their parents. Act out their conversation. **12 minutes**

PURPOSE To develop fluency.

Put the pairs with the same numbers together.

GROUPWORK In groups, the pupils act out their conversation. Get them to practise first and go round and help. Then if there is time, ask some groups to volunteer to act out their conversation in front of the class. This is a fluency exercise so it is best to make a note of any serious mistakes and deal with them at the end or in the next lesson rather than interrupting the conversation as they speak.

Further practice: Activity Book Exercise 5.

ACTIVITY BOOK pages 56 and 57

1 Put the words into the puzzle. Then number the clues. **5 minutes**

Pupils complete the puzzle and number the clues.

2 Look at pages 52 and 56 in your Pupil's Book. Write sentences to complete the story. **15 minutes**

Pupils read the stories again and write sentences to complete the summary.

Answers

2 This is the cave where they slept.
3 This is the restaurant where they had pizza.
4 This is the mountain where the carpet crashed.

Answers

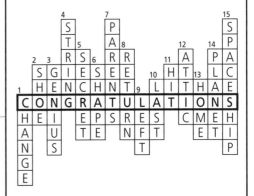

The clues should be numbered reading down: 3, 11, 4, 9, 7, 12, 8, 5, 14, 2, 10, 13, 1, 15, 6

Possible answers

2 The carpet landed on a bridge between two towers.
4 They looked for the card.
6 He tied string to James' shoe and threw it from the bridge.
8 They put the card into the control panel and Laya appeared.
10 The carpet changed into a spaceship.
12 He pushed a blue button and disappeared.

Answers

2 Amy is the girl who is a friend of Max.
3 Max is the boy who had a bad day.
4 Sam is the boy who visited Jack.
5 Jack is the boy who lived in a small town.

Answers

Sentences: 2 = f 3 = d 4 = e 5 = c
6 = a
Pictures: a = 5 b = 6 c = 2 d = 4
e = 1 f = 3

3 Think about the people who you met in this book. Complete the sentences.   10 minutes

Pupils complete the sentences with relative clauses using the words in the box.

4 Make sentences. Match them with the pictures.   12–15 minutes

Pupils match the sentences with relative clauses and number the pictures accordingly.

5 What happened when Gary returned to his planet? Write your ideas. Compare with your friends in the next lesson.   15 minutes

*Note: This activity at the end of the story gives pupils the opportunity to express their own ideas using a range of language. It is more appropriate here to respond to the content of their ideas rather than to the accuracy of what they write. See **A–Z: Fluency** on page 83 and **Writing** on page 93.*

Pupils imagine and write what they think happened when Gary returned to his planet. If pupils do this activity for homework, allow time in the next lesson for them to discuss and compare their ideas.

EXTRA IDEA This piece of work could also be done on a separate piece of paper to go into each pupil's **portfolio**.

6D • Know it all! Brasilia

Topic

The pupils learn about the design and layout of Brasilia. You could have ready more information about this topic (for Pupil's Book Exercises 1b and 2b) and about Rio de Janeiro (for Activity Book Exercise 1). The pupils' project is a creative task but if you have any information about the planning of modern towns, it would be useful.

Project work

The pupils design a new city, making decisions about where to build things and why.

Language

New language
bus station, cathedral, hospital, hotel, in the middle, road, stay, zone

What you need

• Cassette / CD and player.

English Control Panel: *Remind pupils to start completing their English Control Panels for Unit 6.*

Learning skills: *The focus is on listening where the pupils have access to the text of the recording. If they do not have anything suitable at home, you may need to allow class time for this and work with a text from an earlier unit or with a reader which has an accompanying CD or cassette.*

PUPIL'S BOOK pages 58 and 59

 1a Look at the shape of Brasilia from the air. Read about the city and match the pictures with the numbers. | **15 minutes**

PURPOSE To learn about Brasilia and to practise reading intensively.

Pupils read the text carefully and match the pictures with the numbers.

They then compare with a partner. It doesn't matter if they are not sure at this point as the recording in the next exercise will give them the correct answers.

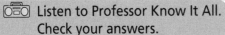 **1b** Listen to Professor Know It All. Check your answers. | **12 minutes**

PURPOSE To practise listening intensively.

Play the recording so that pupils can check what each number refers to. After they have listened, you can then make sure that everyone has matched the pictures correctly.

Further practice: Activity Book Exercises 1 and 2.

Answer key and your notes

Tapescript
Int = *Interviewer*   **Prof** = *Professor*

Int: *Hello and welcome! Today, we are going to talk to Professor Know It All about an amazing city in Brazil. It's the capital, Brasilia. Professor, we have a picture of Brasilia here. It looks like a plane.*

Prof: *Yes, that's right! Brasilia is in the shape of a plane.*

Int: *So Professor, tell me, what are these numbers on the picture?*

Prof: *Yes, the number 1 here ... and here ... are the superblocks. That's where the people live. They live in the wings of the plane. Number 2, here, is the shopping zone. Everything is in zones in Brasilia. And then, next to that, we have another zone, a hotel zone. That's number 3 and here, look, we have **two** hotel zones.*

Int: *This is incredible. It's very organised!*

Prof: *Yes, that's right! Now, in the middle of the body of the plane, number 4, we have a TV tower. And then on the other side, next to the hotel zone, we have the hospital zone, number 5.*

Int: *So, that's 1, 2, 3, 4, and 5. What's number 8?*

Prof: *That's the government zone, in the 'cockpit' of the plane.*

Int: *And numbers 6 and 7?*

1b Tapescript, continued

Prof: *Well, number 7 is the cathedral. It's a very strange building! And number 6 is the bus station.*

Int: *Good, well, thank you, Professor. Can you tell us some more about Brasilia?*

Prof: *Yes, of course. Can you see …*

1b Answers

a hotel = 3   a superblock = 1
a hospital = 5   the shopping zone = 2
a TV tower = 4   the cathedral = 7
the bus station = 6

Answers

1 = b (the superblocks)   2 = d (the schools)
3 = f (the small shops)   4 = e (the big shops)
5 = a (the buildings)   6 = c (the roads)

Answers

2 When the weather is bad.
3 The small shops and schools.
4 You have to drive or take a bus.
5 The architect of / The man who designed Brasilia.
6 Because the roads are very wide / You can get everywhere quickly.

 2a **Listen to Professor Know It All again. Put the topics in the correct order.**   **12 minutes**

PURPOSE To practise listening for gist.

Allow time for pupils to look at the pictures first and then play the recording so pupils can number the topics, either in their books or by writing the letters and numbers in their exercise books. Remind them that they don't need to understand every word for this activity.

Check answers as a whole class.

Tapescript

Int = Interviewer   **Prof** = Professor

Int: *Good, well, thank you, Professor. Can you tell us some more about Brasilia?*

Prof: *Yes, of course. Can you see the superblocks? As I was saying, that's where most people live. They don't live in houses. They live in flats.*

Int: *Oh, here we have a picture of a superblock.*

Prof: *Yes, that's right. The superblocks are up high. They're on legs! This means that children can play under the superblocks if the weather is bad.**

Int: *Where do the children go to school?*

Prof: *Well, the schools and small shops and things like that are all near the superblocks, so people can walk there.**

Int: *What about the big shops?*

Prof: *Well, they are in the shopping zone. If you want to go there, you have to drive or take a bus.**

Int: *Are there a lot of buildings in Brasilia?*

Prof: *Oh yes! Many of the buildings are very exciting. They have unusual shapes and designs. A man called Oscar Niemeyer designed them. He was an architect from Brazil.* But there is also lots of open space – big parks and places for the children.*

Int: *So is it easy to walk around?*

Prof: *Well, it's easy to walk near your superblock.*

Int: *What about the roads?*

Prof: *The roads are very wide. It's excellent if you are in a car because you can get everywhere quickly.**

Int: *Well, thank you, Professor! Brasilia sounds like a very interesting place! And that's all we have time for today. So it's goodbye from me!*

Prof: *And goodbye from me!*

2b **What does the Professor say about Brasilia? Answer the questions.**   **15–20 minutes**

PURPOSE To practise listening intensively.

Allow time for pupils to read the questions and then play the recording again. Play it all through again once and then pausing at the * given in the tapescript for pupils to write down the answers.

Further practice: Activity Book Exercise 3.

Your project

PURPOSE To allow pupils time to develop their own creativity and writing skills.

Pupils can work alone, in pairs or threes for this project. They can design their new city on the computer, or on paper or card, or they can build it with toy building blocks.

Ask them to plan what they should have in a city and write a list of the places. They can think about the shape of the city and where they will put the different places. If they are working in a group, ask them to think about who will do which task. If this is a longer project over a week or two, they could keep a project journal in which they write down who will do what, how, when and where. This will show that everyone is working together as a team.

To accompany the plans and any 3D models, pupils write a description of what there is in their city, where it is and why.

FOLLOW UP Leave time in a future lesson for pupils to present their cities to the rest of the class to generate discussion. Copies of the pupils' plans and explanations and photos of any 3D models can go into each pupil's **portfolio**.

See **A–Z: Project work** on page 90.

ACTIVITY BOOK pages 58 and 59

New vocabulary in Activity Book 6D: get exercise, lie, lifeguard, relax

1 Read about Rio de Janeiro. Think about Brasilia. How are the two cities different?　10 minutes

Pupils read the text and find two more differences.

Answers
Rio is very old.　Rio is by the sea.

2 Find words for each group.　10 minutes

Pupils read the texts again and list vocabulary in different categories.

Suggested answers
1 forests, mountains, beaches, rock, sky
2 different, old, beautiful, fantastic, enormous, famous, bright, unusual
3 playing games, getting exercise, travel by cable car, play music, see fireworks
4 use the beach, relaxing, talking with friends

3 Complete the advice for swimming at the beach.　12 minutes

Pupils complete the advice with words from the box.

Answers
2 there　3 sand　4 water　5 sunglasses
6 red flag　7 long way out　8 dangerous
9 sun　10 yourself

Learning skills: Listening

The learning skills strategy in this unit will help with listening, which pupils often find the most difficult skill, and listening can help pupils learn vocabulary and also improve their pronunciation.

Pupils can do this activity at home, but it is useful to allow time in class to discuss the idea first.

Note: Remind the pupils that many song lyrics are available on the Internet. They may find it useful to learn the word lyrics *for use with a search engine.*

Encourage the pupils to try the activity at home.

English Control Panel

Check that the pupils have completed their English Control Panel for Unit 6, whether in class or at home.

EXTRA IDEA Fast finishers can do further work on their project.

EXTRA PRACTICE There are photocopiable *Extra practice* exercises for this unit on pages 106 and 107. The answers are on page 109.

UNIT TEST There is a photocopiable *Test* for this unit on pages 120 and 121. The tapescript and answers are on page 125.

Revision

Topic
This section contains revision exercises.

Aim
- To revise the language covered in Units 5 and 6.

Language
Revision
Present perfect with *just*
Relative clauses with *who*, *that* and *where*
feel / look / sound / taste like
Past simple and past continuous

Possible answers
Steve has just got off a bus.
Paul has just got on a bus.
Lucy has just taken a photo.
Bill and Ella have just been to the supermarket.
Isabel has just arrived at the supermarket.
Ben has just had a pizza.
Ken and Pat have just stopped / called a taxi.
Ron and Sue have just watched a film / been to the cinema.
Nick has just bought an ice-cream.
Ingrid has just fallen down.
Lina has just talked on the telephone.

Suggested answers
2 This is the shop where they found the control card (in Venice).
3 This is the gondolier who controlled their boat / gondola (in Venice).
4 This is the rope that Alice used / climbed down to get the carpet (on Mount Kenya).
5 This is the tent where they slept (in the Rockies / Rocky Mountains).
6 These are the snakes that Alice / they saw / were in the hole (in the Grand Canyon).
7 This is the girl who gives them the clues.
8 This is the shop where they bought the food, the tent and the torch (near the Rockies / Rocky Mountains).

PUPIL'S BOOK pages 60 and 61

1a Find someone who ... 12 minutes

PURPOSE To develop observation skills.

Pupils can work alone or in pairs for this activity. They look at the picture and find someone for each phrase in the box. There is no need to check answers as the pupils will work in pairs in the next exercise.

1b Work with a friend. Ask and answer. 8 minutes

PURPOSE To revise the present perfect with *just*.

PAIRWORK Pupils work in pairs and take it in turns to ask and answer about people in the picture. Go round and help.

1c Write six sentences about the picture. Make two of them false. Give your sentences to another pair. They find and correct the false ones. 10 minutes

PURPOSE To practise speaking and writing with the present perfect with *just*.

PAIRWORK In pairs, pupils make up and write six sentences about the picture, of which two are false. They exchange them with another pair and find and correct the false sentences.

Note: Activity Book Exercise 2b revises feel / look / smell / sound / taste like but it works on the same dialogue as Exercise 2a. You may prefer pupils to do both these exercises now or as a round-up after Exercise 3b in the Pupil's Book.

Further practice: Activity Book Exercises 2a and 2b.

2 Look at the story again. Find these people, things and places. Write a sentence with 'who', 'that' or 'where'. 15 minutes

PURPOSE To revise relative clauses with *who*, *that* and *where*.

Pupils write a sentence with a relative clause about each of the pictures.

Further practice: Activity Book Exercise 3.

3a What does it look like? Compare ideas with a friend. **7 minutes**

PURPOSE To revise *looks like*.

Pupils look at the pictures and compare ideas with a friend. Check everyone's ideas as a whole class.

3b Complete the questions with the correct words. Follow the lines and complete the answers. **15 minutes**

Pupils work alone and match the questions and answers, adding in the correct words. They then work with a partner and take turns in saying the questions and the answers.

Further practice: Activity Book Exercise 4.

ACTIVITY BOOK pages 60 and 61

1 How well can you remember your English? Put a cross ✗ on the arrow. **8 minutes**

See page 30. After the pupils have put the crosses on the arrows, remind them to start with the exercise that gives them more practice in the area where they feel weakest:

say what someone has just done: Exercise 2a
describe things with 'sounds / looks like', etc.: Exercise 2b
give extra information with 'who / that / where': Exercise 3
talk about the past: Exercise 4

2a Complete the text. **12–15 minutes**

Pupils complete the text with the verbs in the box.

2b Amy is talking to Max about her cake. Complete the conversation. **8 minutes**

Pupils complete the conversation with sense verbs and *like*.

3 Write sentences with 'who', 'that' or 'where'. Draw lines to the pictures. **8 minutes**

Pupils write sentences with relative clauses and draw lines connecting them with the pictures.

4 Read about Tenzing and Hillary's climb. Choose the correct word or write the correct form of the verb. **15 minutes**

Pupils complete the text with different past tense forms.

Answers
It looks like …
1 a bike 2 a cup 3 a can 4 a pencil
5 an apple

Answers
2 look like: No, an alligator has a wider nose.
3 sound like: No, a guitar has strings.
4 look like: No, an African elephant has bigger ears.
5 taste like: No, cola has lots of gas.
6 feel like: No, ice is colder.
7 sound like: No, a bike doesn't have an engine.
8 taste like: No, sugar is sweeter.

Answers
2 has just arrived 3 has just opened
4 has just tasted 5 has just found

Answers
2 smells like 3 feels like 4 tastes like
5 look like 6 look like

Answers
1 … climbed Mount Everest for the first time.
2 This is the place where he stood for the photo.
3 These are the flags that they wanted to fly.
4 This is Edmund Hillary, the man who went with him.
5 This is the tent that they slept in.
6 These are the ropes that they used.
Pupils draw lines to:
Photo A: 1 Tenzing Norgay
2 the ground where he's standing
3 the flags
Photo B: 4 the man on the right
5 the tent behind them 6 the ropes

Answers
2 has just arrived 3 have just made
4 walked 5 stayed 6 started
7 was moving 8 were falling
9 was blowing 10 was getting 11 put
12 camped 13 came 14 was carrying
15 wanted 16 arrived 17 took

Welcome to Alice and James' Fun Park!

ACTIVITY BOOK pages 62 and 63

Note: These activities can be used by fast finishers or as extra revision material.

Suggested answers
When does it open?
When does it close?
How much does it cost?
Where is it?
Is it open in the winter?

1 You want to go to Alice and James' Fun Park. What questions can you ask? **10 minutes**

Pupils write three questions that they could ask about a theme park. Suggested answers are given opposite but the pupils can use any relevant language.

2 What can you do in the park? **10 minutes**

Pupils choose four things to write about. Possible answers are given opposite but the pupils may have other valid ideas based on the picture.

Possible answers
You can: climb a wall   make a snowman
go white water rafting   go swimming
go / travel / ride on a gondola   ski
have a pizza   go to a restaurant
go to a zoo   have a drink / an ice-cream

3 Find three things that are in the wrong place. **5 minutes**

Pupils find and write about the three items that are in the wrong area of the park.

Answers
The J K bridge is in Venice.
The bear is on the Great Wall.
There is a gondola in the Grand Canyon.

4 What have these people just done? **10 minutes**

Pupils find the three people and write what they have just done.

Answers
1 He's just arrived.
2 She's just taken a photo.
3 He's just bought an ice-cream.

5 What were these people doing five minutes ago? **10 minutes**

Pupils find the three people and write what they were doing five minutes ago.

Answers
1 She was climbing the / a wall.
2 He was riding / travelling on a gondola.
3 He was skiing.

6 Where's the carpet? **5 minutes**

Pupils find and write where the carpet is.

7 Which is your favourite part of the park? Why? **8 minutes**

Pupils write which is their favourite part of the park and give a reason.

Answer
It's on Mount Kenya.

A–Z: teaching young learners

Note that words like this: **motivation** indicate a cross-reference within this *A–Z*.

Accuracy

What and why?

Language learning involves a balance of activities which promote both accuracy and **fluency**. At this stage in pupils' language learning most teachers agree that the main aim of learning a language is to encourage communication. Successful written and spoken communication relies on pupils feeling confident. If a large proportion of the language learning activities require pupils to be accurate, they will begin to worry about making **errors** and this will lead to a loss of confidence in fluency and communication. In *Primary Colours 5* there is a combination of accuracy and fluency activities. Maintaining pupils' confidence depends on varying the combinations in each lesson.

Practical ideas

- When planning a lesson look carefully at the activities and note whether they promote accuracy or fluency. Make sure there is a balance of exercises in your lesson – you could write *A* or *F* next to each one. For example, in section 1B, Exercise 1b is an accuracy exercise (the pupils copy a phrase from the box to make each sentence true) and Exercise 1a before that is a fluency exercise as pupils are giving their own ideas.

- Explain to the pupils that there are two kinds of exercise: one where you want them to try and 'get it right' and another when you want them to use their own ideas and experiment both with new words and words they already know. Fluency exercises can be compared with jogging or running when you go at your own speed and accuracy exercises can be compared with playing football when you have to obey the rules.

Acting out

What and why?

Most pupils enjoy the **physical action** involved in drama and role play and there are opportunities throughout the course for the acting out of the stories. Acting out should allow the pupils some freedom so that they can include other language or ideas. Acting out should be a creative, **fluency** task rather than merely a reproductive, or **accuracy**-based one, so that it becomes more personal and memorable.

Practical ideas

- After the pupils have heard the stories, write the key phrases on the board and practise them with the class.

- To help them prepare, assign each pupil a character or let them choose. For example, if there are four characters in the acting out, divide the class into four groups and give each group the same role. In pairs or threes pupils prepare the same characters together so they can support each other. When they are ready each pupil finds pupils who have prepared the roles of the other three characters. They can then prepare their drama together in groups of four.

- If some pupils are shy, ask two pupils to act one role and to take it in turns to speak.

- Encourage the pupils to experiment with working with different classmates.

- Although some pupils may like acting out, others may not like being exposed in front of the class, so it is better to provide other, less public, means of giving these pupils a chance to speak. For example, they may prefer to act out the story sitting down in a small group.

- Watching other pupils act out the story may not be very involving for the rest of the class. It is probably better to limit the acting out to two groups each time and let other groups act out next time. Provide other activities for pupils to do if they seem reluctant to watch.

Additional materials

What and why?

In the language lesson, as in any other lesson, it is always interesting for the pupils to have additional materials to use, refer to or look at.

Practical ideas

- Maps: Maps of your country, region and town are useful. Maps of English-speaking countries such as the UK, the USA, Australia, Canada and New Zealand are all part of learning English. Maps of the world can be used in the unit stories and the D sections.

- Magazine pictures: Collect magazine pictures of the topics in the book. You can use these for extra games and activities.

- Coins: Real or plastic coins from an English-speaking country are very useful for any transactional activities, such as shopping or paying for a meal in a restaurant.

- Readers: Try to get hold of as many English reading books as possible which are appropriate for your pupils. These should not all be fiction – some pupils prefer to read factual information or biographies. Cambridge University Press publishes the *Cambridge Storybooks* which are a delightful series of readers for young learners of English. For more information please see www.cambridge.org/elt/storybooks or get in contact with your local Cambridge University Press representative.

- Websites: You could give pupils addresses of suitable websites for the different topics in the book. Please note that any URLs given in the Teacher's Book are for the convenience of the user and Cambridge University Press assumes no responsibility for their content or functionality.

Assessment

What and why?

There are two kinds of assessment. The first is 'assessment of learning' which gives pupils a mark or grade in a test or a piece of work during the term which forms part of their final grade.

The second is 'assessment *for* learning' which takes place during the lesson. As you go round the class monitoring, helping and observing the pupils working, you will be able to see which ones are having difficulty with certain parts of the lesson. Perhaps one pupil is struggling to spell some words or another hasn't grasped the new grammar point. Have additional materials ready to provide support for the pupils who are weak in certain areas.

Practical ideas

- Assessment *for* learning: When you are preparing the lesson, think ahead to what may be difficult for some pupils, for example, perhaps some of them won't be able to do your planned **writing** task very well. Have ready an alternative support exercise or a different strategy for pupils who may struggle. You could put these pupils in one group and give them some extra help while others work on something else.

- Make a note of which pupil struggles with which aspect of language learning. This will make it easier for you to have ready alternative strategies or teaching ideas.

- Find out from other subject teachers whether the pupils have similar problems in their classes and work on a way of developing a collegial strategy.

- Assessment *of* learning: Most schools will require grades at the end of each term, semester or year to show pupils' progress. If possible, try to give grades for a range of different activities so that pupils have an opportunity to show their strengths. One pupil may be very good at acting out dialogues, for example, but much weaker at the traditional 'filling in the gap' type of test.

- Give grades throughout the semester, so the assessment *of* learning can become included in the assessment *for* learning.

- Make sure the pupils know what the test is testing: language, skills or understanding of the topic area.

- Try to give some tests which test understanding as well as responding. Perhaps one part of the test could ask the pupils to produce questions about a text, rather than answers.

Brainstorming

What and why?

'Brainstorming' is the term used to describe ways of collecting ideas together. This can be done as a whole class activity or in groups or pairs or even individually.

Practical ideas

- Each of the units in *Primary Colours 5* is set in a different country, and different places (in that country or linked thematically with the place in the Pupil's Book) are mentioned in the Activity Book. Before reading about the place in the book you could do some brainstorming with the class to find out what pupils already know or what they would like to know about each place. It is often better to do this first in small groups or pairs and then write the ideas as a whole class on the board together.

- Pupils in pairs and groups may brainstorm in MT but you can put their ideas on the board in English as a way of providing vocabulary for the topic.

Classrooms

What and why?

Most pupils spend most of their daytime hours in uninviting classrooms. A stimulating and inviting classroom environment can have a significant effect on the achievement levels of pupils, on their attitude, and on their **discipline** and **motivation**.

It is not always easy to decorate a classroom if you are not in the same room all the time so the suggestions below fall into two categories.

Practical ideas for the same room

- Involve the pupils in making decisions about how you decorate the classroom. Perhaps they can bring in posters, etc. to put on the walls.

- **Displaying pupils' work** is important. Make sure that everyone's work is put up on the display boards at some time.

- Try to create different 'corners' in the classroom, thus making smaller areas where the pupils can feel comfortable. For example, a **reading** corner, a **writing** corner, and a **listening** corner.

- Make a display area. The pupils could bring in things which they can show to the other pupils and tell them about. You could have a display that relates to the unit theme in *Primary Colours 5*, for example, pictures of fossils or snakes for Unit 1.

Practical ideas for different rooms

- Put a cloth over your desk, or hang something on the wall, to try to create a different feeling for the English classes.

- Hang a string from one side of the room to the other and use clothes pegs to hang pieces of work from it during the lesson.

- **Music** can also be important in establishing a welcoming classroom atmosphere.

Content-based language learning

What and why?

Many teachers are now drawing on other parts of the school curriculum and beyond to give content to the language lessons. In addition to learning the grammar and **vocabulary** of the language, pupils can use knowledge and skills from other lessons in the English lesson. One advantage of this is that pupils who may find English more difficult can draw on their expertise from other areas, and this increases their **motivation**. The other advantage is that this makes links across the curriculum and deepens pupils' understanding of, and involvement in, the topic, particularly when they are doing **project work**. It also broadens the vocabulary base of the pupils.

All levels of *Primary Colours* have touched on other areas of the curriculum and in *Primary Colours 4* and *5* these links are made particularly strongly in the *Know it all!* sections (section D).

Practical ideas

- While preparing the unit, ask other colleagues if they have taught the topic so that you have an idea of what the pupils may already know.

- Ask other colleagues if they have information which you can borrow – perhaps some pictures or maps or references which you and the pupils can use for additional material or project work.

- Take time to look at the pupils' textbooks from other subject areas so that you have an idea of what they may already know. It may be possible for some of the project work and **portfolio** work to combine English with one or more other subjects.

- The language lesson can provide a springboard for a new topic which pupils can study in more depth later in MT in another subject lesson or it can consolidate topics already studied in other subject lessons.

- Try to find appropriate websites for the pupils to refer to.

- Look around the local area for museums and exhibitions which may be interesting for the pupils to visit or which may lend you materials for the topic.

- Find out if any of the parents are specialists in the topic area and if they would like to come and talk to the pupils in more detail.

Discipline

What and why?

Often, discipline 'problems' seem to increase as the pupils go up through school. We cannot expect 100% attention all the time from young pupils – partly because not all activities will match some pupils' strengths and interests.

Flexibility, patience and a variety of activities will usually improve pupils' attention and avoid feelings of failure. In some cases, however, real discipline problems arise. In the language lesson the most common reason for this is boredom. Pupils become bored if:

- the activities are predictable and unvaried.

- they don't have an opportunity to initiate their own ideas and language.

- they are not allowed to draw on their own strengths and talents.

- the overall emphasis of the lessons is on 'getting it right' (**accuracy**).

- they cannot make choices and decisions about the way they work.

- they don't feel they are making progress.

- they don't get help with an area of weakness.

- their efforts are not noticed.

Practical ideas

- Keep clear records which show each pupil's strengths and weaknesses. An overall mark for a piece of **writing** may not help the pupil who is struggling with spelling or punctuation or a particular grammar point. When marking written work, have a separate sheet with key headings. If a pupil has a 'weak' spot, make a note on the sheet and then provide extra activities which will help with that area. This will encourage the pupils to identify their strengths and weaknesses, for example, *I'm not very good at spelling but my punctuation is OK*.

Name	Tom	Anna	Jane	Nick
Spelling	X			X
Grammar		X		
Punctuation			X	
Vocabulary				
Creativity				X

- Keep records of how pupils respond to different kinds of activities. Which pupils enjoy singing, drama, cutting and sticking, **reading**, bringing extra things into class, drawing, working on a computer? Pupils are often disruptive because there are not enough opportunities in the lesson for them to use their hands and bodies. Offer them more of the activities which they prefer.

- Many pupils find it hard to 'learn'. When you ask the class to prepare for a **vocabulary** test, always provide them with ways in which they can learn their words. Ask them to discuss in groups or class what they do to learn their vocabulary and collect the ideas on the board. Add ideas of your own which encourage pupils to make something in order to help them learn. For example, they can make a puzzle by choosing a word and writing or drawing clues to make other words from the different letters in the word. Or they can write an 'odd one out' exercise, or split words in half. Before pupils do a task, ask them to tell you which strategies they are using to help them learn. Then at the end of the activity, ask them if their strategies were successful or if they will try something else next time. In section D of the Activity Book there are suggestions for different learning strategies.

- If the pupils need a grade at the end of term, semester or year, encourage them to work towards a **portfolio** grade. This encourages pupils to discuss their work and progress with you.

- Try to give disruptive pupils a key role in classroom management. Perhaps they can help you carry all your equipment to and from the classroom and put the cassettes and CDs back in their cases. Perhaps they can stick finished work and posters on the walls. Perhaps you can form an 'entertainments committee' which works out the songs, plays and work that can be shown to the parents one evening a year / term. The committee can make a programme for the event. Perhaps they can help you choose new readers for next year and help look after the classroom library. The aim is to bring the disruptive pupil into the *process* of the language lesson and draw attention away from the *product* which many pupils find threatening.

Displaying pupils' work

What and why?

At the end of each of the six units pupils will have produced a piece of **project work**. To give them a sense of pride and purpose in their work, it is a good idea to display it.

Practical ideas

- Put their work on the classroom wall for a week or so and then change it.

- Take some photos of the pupils' work and display them instead if there is not much room in the classroom.

- If you can't use the classroom for display, ask if you can display work in the school corridors, canteen, library or entrance hall.

- You may be able to display pupils' work in a more public space – for example, the town library, Tourist Information bureau or hotel foyer.

- Pupils, or the teacher in charge of the school website if necessary, could put the work on the school website for other schools to see.

Education

What and why?

At this age, whether pupils are learning English in school alongside other curriculum subjects or in a language institution after school, learning a foreign language is part of their education. Pupils bring expectations and experience of learning to English language lessons. The activities of the language lesson are well suited to developing skills which can be used across their education, such as learning to work in groups, finding out information, evaluating progress, reflecting on ways of working, comparing, using imagination and asking questions. The topic-based content of the units expects and encourages pupils to draw on information from other subject-based areas and to combine the information in different ways using the new structures and **vocabulary** of English. This serves to make the lessons both memorable and motivating.

Practical ideas

- Encourage the pupils to ask questions about the topic and not merely to answer them.
- Help pupils think of ways to find out more information and research a topic to find answers.
- Encourage pupils to use a range of reference materials, for example, encyclopaedias, maps, atlases, CD-Roms, websites and the library.
- Encourage pupils to become individual 'experts' in a particular area of the topic and to share their knowledge with the class.
- If you teach other subjects to the same class, try to use some of the English from English lessons in, for example, the History lessons.

English and the mother tongue

What and why?

Traditionally, teachers have been encouraged to use only English in the language classroom and by the fifth year of learning English much of the classroom language is probably English. However, it is important to continue to use MT (the mother tongue) if possible to provide extra support for pupils who do not understand a task, especially if it is the first time they have done a particular activity. It is also useful to use MT during project work and before starting a new game to ensure that the pupils understand what they have to do. The use of mother tongue allows for a wider range of activities in the classroom which encourages the sense of involvement with the language and learning. It is important for pupils to be able to ask for help, explain problems and say how they feel in their own language.

Practical ideas

- Give instructions in English, but repeat them again in MT if this is a new type of activity.
- In the project activities, show the pupils what to do and use language of *explanation* rather than *instruction*.
- Explain in English, but allow time for the pupils to 'process' the language before the next explanation. Pupils understand more when they have time to think between statements.
- When pupils are discussing ideas in pairs or groups, be aware that they will probably use MT.

English Control Panel

What and why?

At the end of the *Welcome!* unit of the Activity Book, pupils use Cut-outs 1 and 2 (from pages 127 and 128) to make an English Control Panel which they use throughout the book. After each unit, the pupils complete their English Control Panel as a record of learning to help them remember new **vocabulary**, grammar and the topic and focus of the story.

Practical ideas

- The Activity Book reminds about the English Control Panel at the end of each unit, but you can encourage the pupils to complete them as they work through each section and come across different topics and language.
- Pupils can keep their English Control Panels at home to be a regular part of their homework activities, but ask them to bring them into class sometimes so that they can compare them with each other. Pupils always like looking at others' work.
- Ask individually if they want their English Control Panel to be included in their **portfolio**.
- You can keep an English Control Panel yourself and show it to the pupils from time to time.
- Encourage pupils to write reflections (in MT) about their progress in English.

Errors

What and why?

All pupils will make errors while they are learning English (and when acquiring their own language). It is only through making errors and then hearing or seeing the correct form that their own understanding of how English works is developed. It takes considerable time, and practice, to produce language correctly. Some of the activities in *Primary Colours 5* are designed to help pupils produce correct language and some are designed to help them experiment with language. Over-correction of errors at this experimental stage will probably make the pupils less confident about speaking English because they will be frightened of 'making a mistake'.

Practical ideas

- Decide whether an exercise is designed to encourage **fluency** or **accuracy**.

- Correct the activity accordingly. If it is an accuracy exercise, explain this in advance to the pupils and correct them as they work through the exercise. If it is a fluency exercise, listen and correct the main errors afterwards.

- Limit yourself to correcting only the key errors as they speak or write.

- Encourage pupils to correct their own **writing** by giving them a list of things to check before they hand in their work for correction, for example spelling, tenses, articles, plurals, prepositions (STAPP).

- The Learning skills section in Unit 4 of the Activity Book focuses on the strategy of pupils identifying and correcting errors in their written work.

Evaluation

What and why?

Evaluation in *Primary Colours 5* encourages pupils to consider how they are learning and where they need extra help and support. The *Revision and evaluation* sections after Units 2, 4 and 6 in the Activity Book ask pupils to look back at the language of the previous two units and to reflect on their progress.

Practical ideas

- Pupils who used *Primary Colours 4* will be familiar with the idea of self-evaluation. However, at the beginning, any pupils who have not been introduced to the idea may not take self-evaluation or reflection very seriously. This may be because they don't know how to reflect on their learning or because they don't see its relevance. Give them time in class to reflect on what they are best at and what they are weakest at.

- At the end of some activities, leave time to ask them to think about how well they have understood the new language and what strategies worked best to help them understand.

- Encourage pupils to talk about how they learn new grammar and **vocabulary**. Many pupils think that everybody learns in the same way.

- Give them some examples from your own life where you have evaluated and reflected.

Fluency

What and why?

The activities in *Primary Colours* are a balance between **accuracy** (where the pupils are encouraged to try and get the answers right) and fluency exercises which encourage the pupils to initiate their own ideas and language. In these activities pupils will make **errors** and stumble for unknown words. This is part of the process of building up the confidence needed for successful communication.

Practical ideas

- Fluency activities, such as *What do you think of ...?* or *Would you like to ...?* will often create the need for new language. Words which the pupils have needed to use themselves will be remembered better than words given to them.

- If pupils make a mistake in a fluency exercise, don't correct them directly, just repeat the sentence accurately.

- When pupils speak during a fluency activity, respond to the content of what they are saying rather than to the correctness of the statement. Over-correction during fluency work will lead to a lack of confidence.

- Make sure the pupils know when they are doing a fluency activity. You can say something like, *I'm interested in hearing your ideas about this topic. Don't worry if you make a mistake – your opinions are the most important thing now.*

Games

What and why?

Games are a very important part of a successful route to language learning for young learners. They are useful in a number of ways: in maintaining **motivation**, in giving a natural context for using English and in providing variety within a lesson.

Practical ideas

- While the pupils will enjoy the 'game' aspect of the activity, it is important that they understand that it is not just for fun. Explain for example, *Let's play a game to help us remember the new words.*

- The *Games extra* section in this Teacher's Book includes some notes on using games and some games that you can play with the class.

- It is important to ensure that *all* the pupils understand how to play the game. Explain in **English and the mother tongue** and then get the pupils to tell you how to play the game.

- After you have played a game successfully, you can ask the pupils to suggest variations on the game, or to suggest new games. You could have a 'suggestion box' in class for this.

- Include a game in different parts of the lesson – not always at the end. A game shouldn't be seen as a 'reward' for hard work, but another way of learning.

- After the pupils have played a game, ask them if they liked it, how they could play it better, or how they would improve on it.

- Board games are a useful way of revising language. You can ask the pupils to make their own board game.

Homework

What and why?

Homework helps pupils reinforce what they have been learning in class and can prepare them for the next lesson.

Practical ideas

- Small amounts of homework are best – perhaps twenty minutes' work should be the target at this age. More than that may make pupils react negatively to their learning.

- The Activity Book provides many exercises which can be done for homework. However, before asking pupils to work on exercises at home, go through the exercises first so they are very clear about what to do and when to do it.

- If you take in pupils' Activity Books and mark their written work at home, spend some time going through their work in class so that the pupils can learn from the corrections rather than just getting a grade.

- Vary the kind of homework which pupils do. It is useful to have homework as follow-up reinforcement work but it is also useful to have some homework which asks pupils to look ahead to the work for the next lesson. For example, ask them to read the story before the lesson, or to find three new words on the next page, or to bring something to the lesson which relates to the next topic.

- Give pupils a choice of homework exercises. For example, *You can do Exercise 1 or 2 on page 20*, or if there are ten questions in one exercise ask them to choose to answer six. These choices help with involvement.

Language development

What and why?

Different pupils learn at different rates. This may be partly natural, although in many cases, it may be possible to improve a pupil's rate of learning by changes in the **classroom**, and by thinking about **motivation** and levels of **participation**. With most learners, children or adults, there is a natural gap between their ability to *comprehend* and their ability to *produce*. (This is usually true for their first language as well.) Some researchers have suggested that learners go through a 'silent period' in the early stages of the process and they therefore advise teachers not to 'push' pupils to speak. Most of this research, however, concerns learners arriving in a new culture, where they may feel overwhelmed by the total change in their lives. In primary classrooms, there may be many other reasons why a pupil is silent, which have very little to do with 'natural' development.

Practical ideas

- Pupils can be silent because they feel shy or lack confidence in front of others. Try to encourage them to speak and help them produce the language in a smaller group where they don't feel so exposed.

- Language learning is a slow process that does not go in a straight line. We should not expect mastery of one language form before the pupils move on to another teaching / learning area. Many **errors** remain even up to 'advanced' levels (for example, the absence of a third person *-s* in *She works*, etc.). Expect errors in the pupils' language production as a natural part of the learning process.

- Different pupils will develop their language ability at different rates and in different areas. Some may find it more difficult to speak than others, while they are stronger in **reading** or **writing**. It is important to continue to encourage the pupils to *try*, but it takes time to develop confidence.

- Some pupils may feel that they are not learning anything. Help them to see how much they have learned by keeping examples of their work in **portfolios** or by recording them speaking.

Large classes

What and why?

Large classes of 25+ pupils require careful classroom management to ensure that pupils are involved in the tasks, can hear the recording, and also see the board and you! It is important to find ways of 'breaking down' the size of a large class and to make personal contact more possible. This is especially important when some pupils in the class may have poor eyesight, may be slightly deaf or have other **special needs**.

Practical ideas

- As far as possible, ask pupils to work in pairs and groups. **Pairwork and groupwork** allow you the opportunity to spend some time with those pupils who may be in need of extra support. At the beginning of sections A and C ask pupils to read the episode of the story silently in pairs first and to discuss new words. Go round and listen to how the pupils tackle the process of working out meaning from picture or context clues. Then ask two pairs or a group of three to work together and to read the story each taking the role of one of the characters. Go round and listen to as many groups as you can.

- In a large class some pupils will finish an exercise before the others. Have additional work ready for the fast finishers. This will give you more time to go round and help the slower pupils.

- It is often better to avoid classroom discussions in a large class because only a few pupils may offer the ideas and suggestions while the rest of the class stays quiet and uninvolved because they can't hear clearly what the others are saying.

- For **brainstorming** in large classes, ask pupils to work in groups and then ask the groups to say one idea each which you can write on the board.

- **Songs**, **project work** and drama all generate noise. If you need to talk to a pupil when the class is working rather noisily, approach the pupil and speak quietly. Pupils' noise will always rise above a teacher's shouting.

- If you would like to have the attention of the whole class, it is worth having a word combined with an action which you can say quietly (perhaps say *Control card!* and put your hand up). When pupils hear this word and see this action, they will know they should stop what they are doing and listen to you.

Listening

What and why?

Many of the activities in *Primary Colours* are based around the pupils listening to the recording as a stimulus for speaking activities afterwards. Many pupils find listening to the recordings difficult – they may suffer from minor deafness or the room may be noisy. Many problems of **discipline** and **motivation** often stem from the fact that pupils can't hear the recording clearly.

Practical ideas

- Sit at the back of the class and check whether the recording is loud enough.

- Listening at this level is generally a *means* of helping the pupils learn the language. If listening activities are used as a *goal* of language learning, they are supported with questions or a table to fill in which helps pupils' listening.

- Listening in a foreign language is very difficult and many pupils need the support of pictures, pre-reading the text, or to have the text in front of them. Limit the number of listening activities which the pupils do without this support.

- If pupils listen to an episode of the story without the text, pause the recording between frames and ask pupils to write down some key words they have heard to give them a framework or you could write some key words for each frame on the board first to guide them through the listening.

- Ask pupils to listen in pairs or groups and then to share their ideas about the text afterwards.

Mixed abilities

What and why?

Pupils bring different experiences and expectations with them to school. The larger the class, the greater these differences may appear, and because of these differences we cannot expect that all the pupils will be interested in or able to do the same tasks in the same way at the same time. A poor ability in English often means that the pupil is not responding well to specific activity types – it doesn't mean that s/he cannot learn.

Practical ideas

- Not all pupils will work or learn at the same pace. It is useful to have extra puzzles or exercises ready for fast finishers. These can be written by the pupils – when the pupils have completed an exercise, particularly in the Activity Book, they can create another similar exercise for other pupils. They can write the answers on the back and place it in a Puzzle Box. Pupils can take a puzzle or exercise from the Puzzle Box to complete while they are waiting.

- Particularly in **large classes**, it is important to have regular personal contact with the pupils. This will help you find out if they are keeping up with the rest of the class. Make sure you discuss the pupils' **portfolios** with them regularly.

- At the end of each unit, allow time for the pupils to sit in small groups and go through what they have learned. You could form groups to make sure that some of the less able pupils are placed with the more able. Ask them to write an exercise about the unit which they can give to another group to do as a test.

- Some pupils prefer to learn by **writing** and drawing. Others prefer to learn by handling objects. Try to increase the number of manipulative activities which the pupils can do in class. Perhaps they can use plasticine to make figures of the characters which they can move around as they listen to the story.

- Encourage pupils to bring items or ideas from home which link in with the units.

- The aim is to help all pupils feel confident about language learning so it is better to wait until the individual pupil is ready before pushing them to speak or **act out** drama in English.

Motivation

What and why?

Initially, the motivation of young learners is generally very high. Often by the fifth year of learning English many pupils lose their motivation. One of the reasons for the drop in motivation is that some pupils are anxious about making **errors**, which has a negative effect on their self-esteem. It is therefore important that the activities the pupils do in class create feelings of success, not failure. Pupils are often more motivated if they have been able to make decisions about what they can do, for example, about the inclusion of work in their **portfolios**.

Practical ideas

- Try to ensure that the pupils have a clear idea of how much they have learned and a feeling that they are making progress. For example, ask them to look back at the work they were doing a month or so ago and say things like, *Look! One month ago you couldn't understand that. Now you can!*

- Larger tasks such as projects can create a feeling of more personal control.

- Plan activities which the pupils can take pride in. Some pupils may want to play the guitar or piano when the others are singing the **songs**. You may want to work with the music teacher to make a class choir which sings the English songs for a school concert with other pupils playing instruments or dancing.

- **Displaying pupils' work** in a classroom may not be possible but you may be able to negotiate with the headteacher to have an 'English corridor' where you can put up work. Pupils find it very motivating to have work on display.

- Think of other places outside school where you can display work. For example, the work on designing a new city could be displayed in the town museum. Ask the pupils to help you think of different places to 'show off' their work.

- Find out what the pupils think. For example, find out if they think they need more practice, or if they have suggestions of their own. You could place a 'Suggestion Box' in your class, or write a guided letter that the pupils could complete with their ideas.

- Try to think of ways in which the pupils can be encouraged to make choices. This may be a choice of materials to use in a project, a choice of whether they do something in **writing** or orally, a choice of how long they will spend on a particular task, a choice of what they do for homework, a choice of where they sit in the classroom, and so on.

- Increase positive, encouraging feedback which emphasises the importance of the *process* or progress not only of the *product* of their work.

Music

What and why?

Music can help to establish a classroom 'atmosphere', it can make learning more memorable and it can give a sense of security and comfort to the pupils. **Songs** are very useful in developing confidence for some learners in English and giving practice, but instrumental music can also be used to great effect in the classroom.

Practical ideas

- If you play music when you are **starting a lesson**, you can help ease the pupils into their English lesson and make the 'psychological switch' from what they were doing immediately before.

- Different types of music can be used to affect the pace that the pupils are working at. If, for example, they are doing **project work**, you could play some soft, classical music which will encourage them to work with care. If you want them to work more quickly, you can choose faster, more rhythmic music.

- You can choose a variety of music as a background – for example, classical music, pop music, South American pipe music or Indian music. You could just briefly tell the pupils the name of the type of music and where it comes from.

- You could select different types of music from English-speaking countries: classical music, folk music, pop music, old music, modern music, etc.

- You could ask the pupils to suggest music.

Pairwork and groupwork

What and why?

The time that pupils spend in English lessons is usually quite short. Working in pairs or small groups means that more pupils have more opportunity to talk more. More importantly groupwork in small groups or pairwork gives them the space to digest new language, to exchange ideas and to be creative. It can provide a change of pace and variety. Whole class work, especially with a **large class**, demands a lot of attention and concentration in one 'mode' – more than most pupils are able to give.

It is important to provide opportunities for small groupwork or pairwork, but it is equally important to remember that different kinds of pairwork and groupwork require different input and skills by the pupils. For pupils to get the most out of their pairwork and groupwork activities it is important that you spend a little time beforehand setting up the tasks clearly.

Practical ideas

- Before the pupils work in pairs or groups, make sure they know exactly what they have to do. You can give the instructions in both **English and the mother tongue**.

- Some pairwork and groupwork activities ask the pupils to practise new language. This is an **accuracy** exercise so it may be useful to give an example before starting by asking one or two pupils to do the exercise in front of the class. Then while they are working, you can go around the class, listening and helping.

- It is usually best to limit the time for pairwork and to let pupils know how long they have. If you allow too much time, they will lose the focus and not see the point of what they are doing. It is equally important that you don't allow too little time. This can cause frustration and confusion.

- Ensure that any work you ask pupils to do in pairs has a concrete focus – that it is clear to them what *you* expect. Some **fluency** tasks ask them to share ideas. Make sure pupils know that you expect them to give you these ideas at the end of the activity.

- Some pupils will certainly finish before others. In this case, have short extra exercises available. The Activity Book exercises and the Extra practice exercises or the extra puzzles or exercises in the Puzzle Box can be used for this purpose.

- You could make a timetable of when you will talk personally to each group, perhaps while the other pupils are getting on with some other work. A key factor in pupils' success is if someone cares that they are learning. Personal contact and interest in pupils' work is extremely important.

- Groups can have a representative. The other pupils can then tell their representative if they have suggestions, want extra practice, etc. See **Large classes**.

Participation

What and why?

Pupils can have very different levels of participation in the classroom. Some pupils may appear not to participate at all, while others are very active. Part of the reason for this may be that pupils are learning in different ways. Some pupils prefer to learn quietly, by themselves, while others like to work in a group or pair, and enjoy the social contact through working. As long as the pupils work towards the goals that you have set, it is usually best to tolerate different ways of working where this is possible. It is vital that the pupils feel happy in the classroom and the social aspect of this is important. Some researchers have suggested that as a part of their **language development** pupils naturally go through a 'silent period' when they are learning a foreign language.

Practical ideas

- Try to talk to the pupils individually and find out how they prefer to work. You should be able to find out if they prefer to work alone or in pairs. See **Pairwork and groupwork**.

- Some pupils are easily distracted if they work in pairs, and achieve very little. In this case, try to sit them with someone else who works more seriously and see if that helps. If that doesn't work any better, you can give them a chance to work alone.

- Some pupils are naturally quiet in the classroom, but they achieve good results. Other pupils are quiet because they feel shy in front of others or afraid to speak. Try to adopt an encouraging attitude and tell them that they can do it if they just try!

- Pupils who do not participate very much often sit at the back of the classroom. This can increase their feeling of being 'removed from the action'. It is generally a good idea to move the pupils around regularly, so that all the pupils have a chance to sit near the front. Often, you will notice dramatic differences in their levels of participation if you do this.

Physical action

What and why?

Physical movement is very important in a number of ways for young learners. Pupils at this age need to move – it is through physical movement and contact that they develop a fuller experience of the world. In language learning, we can harness this fact to help learning become 'deeper' and more memorable for the pupils. Physical action does not always need a lot of space: pupils can move while standing at their desks.

Practical ideas

- Start the lesson with some physical activity, for example, a song with actions.

- If you want pupils to **act out** a story, encourage them to include *action* in it. That is, not just saying the words, but moving arms, legs, making gestures, miming actions, etc.

- If the pupils are repeating some words after you, make an action which they can copy while they say the word.

- Mime is also a useful way to include physical action. If a pupil mimes a series of actions, perhaps ones that come from one of the stories in the course, the other pupils can say what the words are that go with the actions.

Portfolios

What and why?

A portfolio is a selection of a pupil's work collected over a term, semester or school year. The purpose of the portfolio, at this age, is to provide a tangible record of a pupil's progress and to give the pupil an opportunity to reflect on his / her work.

Practical ideas

- The first time you introduce portfolio work to the pupils, explain that they can collect their work in a file or drawer and choose 4–6 pieces to keep at the end of the term.

- Explain how the portfolio works in MT.

- Encourage pupils to improve or add to their work during the term.

- Ask pupils to choose different kinds of work to go in their portfolio, for example drawings, **writing**, cassettes / CDs / MP3s, craft work.

- Allow time for the pupils to look at other pupils' portfolio work during the term.

- Allow time to discuss with the pupils how they can improve certain pieces of work.

Previewing

What and why?

It is helpful for all pupils if they know what they are going to be doing in the lesson.

Practical ideas

- You can preview by telling the pupils what they will be doing that lesson. For example, *Today, we're going to read the next part of the story and then learn a new song.*

- You can ask the pupils to look for certain things in the book, for example, to find the song at the back of the book, or to find an exercise where they will work in pairs.

- You can preview at the beginning of a week, at the beginning of a lesson and – if there are many steps involved (for example, in sections A and C) – before the pupils start an activity.

Project work

What and why?

At the end of the D sections, pupils have the opportunity to work on projects. These are designed to extend the topic of the unit and to help them learn language by bringing other strengths to the language classroom. Pupils who may find it more difficult than others to learn new vocabulary and grammar may excel at project work and be able to take a leading role in helping others. This opportunity can have a significant impact on motivation.

The project work in *Primary Colours 5* aims to:
- help the pupils with **writing** in English
- increase confidence
- encourage creativity
- develop collaborative skills
- foster the ability to work independently

Practical ideas

- Before the lesson, look ahead to see what the topic of the project work is so that you can collect reference materials and website addresses for the pupils.

- Pupils can work alone or in pairs or small groups for their projects.

- Decide which would be the best lesson in the week to set aside for the project. Some or even most of the project work can be done for homework but it is probably a good idea to start the project off in class so pupils can work out what they are going do, who they will work with and what they will produce.

- Make sure that pupils know what they are expected to do and when you want it to be finished.

- When pupils are planning their project, encourage them to think about how they will find materials, who in the group is responsible for each part of it and how and where they will work together.

- Decide on the best way of **displaying pupils' work**. Displays can be in a variety of places and it is worth asking pupils for their ideas as this will increase their **motivation**. Within the school, displays can be made along corridors, in libraries and in canteens as well as in the classroom. There are often places outside schools in the town which enjoy having a temporary display. Once the pupils realise that their work can be displayed outside their school, they will generate lots of ideas for suitable places!

- It is important that you leave some classroom time for the **evaluation** process. This is done in MT and allows the pupils a chance to reflect on what they learned and how they learned it. Projects encourage pupils to work together as well as independently and pupils may find that both these ways of working are more demanding than they may be used to. During the time for evaluation you could ask them to think about these and other similar questions:
  - What did you learn from doing your project?
  - What did you find easiest / hardest to do?
  - Is there anything you would change if you did a similar project again?
  - What were the good / bad things about working in a pair / group?

Reading

What and why?

By now, most, but possibly not all, pupils will be able to read the texts in *Primary Colours 5* with confidence. Some pupils may have reading problems in MT and these may be transferred to the English lessons.

Practical ideas

- Pupils work in pairs or groups and read out the story texts from sections A and C to each other. Encourage them to help each other with difficult words. In large classes it is less threatening for weaker pupils to read to a small group. Go round and help and note which pupils are having difficulties.
- Cambridge University Press publishes the *Cambridge Storybooks* which are a delightful series of readers for young learners of English. For more information please see www.cambridge.org/elt/storybooks or get in contact with your local Cambridge University Press representative.

- Give weaker pupils more reading practice with texts they find interesting. These may not be fiction texts. Ask the weaker pupils what they are interested in – perhaps football, or pop songs. Share the responsibility with individual pupils to find texts in English which reflect his / her interests. Texts which the pupils enjoyed reading, for example, texts about famous footballers or the words of a pop song, can then go in their **portfolios**.
- Encourage all pupils to read each other's **writing**.
- Pair dictation exercises often help weaker readers. Pupils dictate what they have written to their partner.
- Encourage weaker pupils to keep their own flashcards of words or vowel / consonant clusters which they find difficult to read. These can go in their portfolios.

Songs

What and why?

The songs have been specially written for the course. They give the pupils **listening** practice and help them to practise the new structures and **vocabulary**.

Practical ideas

- Some pupils are not naturally musical or perhaps are slightly deaf. They will respond better to being allowed to hum or 'la la' the tune to help them learn the melody. They can then add the words later.

- When the pupils know a song, ask them to work in pairs to sing it together – perhaps every alternate line.
- Where possible, you could encourage the pupils to make up new words for the song.

Special needs

What and why?

All pupils are 'special', of course, and every pupil has needs which teachers need to take into account. The phrase 'special needs', however, is normally used to refer to pupils who have particular learning needs which are identified by the school system and for which extra support is provided. In many cases, however, the difficulties that a pupil suffers may go unnoticed. These may include partial deafness, limited vision, reading difficulties, restlessness or hyperactivity. Although English teachers are not normally qualified to make judgements about

the special needs of a pupil, they can have a role in identifying the help or attention a pupil may need.

Practical ideas

- One of the most common problems in large classes is partial deafness. Many more pupils now suffer from 'glue ear' and this will disadvantage them when they need to listen closely to the recording. You may be able to put the cassette / CD player in the middle of the room rather than at the front to help these pupils hear better.

- Give pupils with hearing problems ample time to look at the pictures and read the story before listening to the recording. Pupils will be demotivated very quickly if they cannot hear the recording when they are asked to listen with books closed. Rather than singling pupils out, give the whole class a choice by saying, *You can keep your books open or closed while you listen to the story.*

- It is often useful to tell pupils what you plan to do next lesson so this gives them time to look ahead and be prepared.

- As far as possible, keep activities short. Six or seven minutes may be the maximum attention span of a lot of pupils at this age. Break up the task into smaller sections with a different emphasis.

Starting a lesson

What and why?

The first moments of a lesson can establish for a pupil how far they feel 'included' and whether they will understand what is happening. Building this bridge into the lesson is often the key factor in whether the lesson is successful for some pupils or not.

Practical ideas

- Try to start by asking pupils what they can remember about the last lesson. The replies do not have to be about the 'content' of the lesson – the new structures or **vocabulary** – but anything they can think of, for example, *It was raining, The class next door was noisy* or *It was Peter's birthday.* Accept every answer – this is a confidence and **fluency** activity not an **accuracy** one. Getting the pupils themselves to contribute to the beginning of the lesson will help them 'switch into' English.

- Ask pupils if anyone has found out any information about the topic and plan when you and the class can hear about it or see it.

- You can play one of the songs they know as they come into the class.

- Ask pupils to look back at the pages they have done in the book and find certain things, for example, a picture of a gondola, two of Laya's codes, a picture of Gary, three words beginning with *s* and two words beginning with *t*.

- 'Show and tell' is a good way to start a lesson, making the pupils feel personally involved. For example, you can ask the pupils to bring in an item that has something to do with the topic.

Stories

What and why?

Stories provide an ideal focus and context for English and, at the same time serve to broaden the pupils' view of the world and their place in it. Firstly, the language of the story is presented in a recognisable situation and allows for the natural recycling of language. Secondly, stories provide an excellent opportunity for extensive **listening**. Thirdly, stories also allow pupils to identify with the place – or setting – through visual clues.

Practical ideas

- Before listening to the story ask the pupils to look closely at the pictures so they can have a rough idea of what happens. They can then close their books and listen to the story without reading the text.

- When they have heard the story once, ask a few questions in MT to check that they have understood. These can be more 'open' rather than 'closed'

questions to allow pupils the opportunity to think of individual responses, for example, *Would you like to visit the Grand Canyon? Would you like to travel on the carpet?*

- There are thirteen episodes of the story in *Primary Colours 5* (one in the *Welcome!* unit and two in each of the following six units). Try to plan some different ways for the pupils to approach the pictures and text. You could ask pupils to listen to the story sometimes with their books open and sometimes with their books closed; read the text sometimes before hearing the story and sometimes afterwards; read the story out loud to each other in pairs before or after listening to the recording. Alternatively, you could read the story to them yourself before playing the recording.

Vocabulary

What and why?

At this stage, vocabulary is probably the most important part of the language learning process for moving into independence. Pupils can communicate reasonably effectively with a large vocabulary even if their grammatical competence is still weak. One problem of vocabulary learning is that pupils learn new words from one unit by rote which are quickly forgotten during the next unit.

Practical ideas

- There are new words in each story. It may be more involving for the pupils if you let them hear or read the story first before focusing on new vocabulary.

- As far as possible, allow time for the pupils to ask about new vocabulary after they have tried to work out the meaning rather than offering it to them first. You can do this with a 'traffic light' system in which each pupil has a red, green and orange crayon. They underline or write in their exercise books any new words in green which they can guess from the story; then they underline or write in orange any new words which they can guess but which they are still unsure about; finally, they underline or write in red any words which they don't understand at all. Get them to compare the words on their lists with a partner or in small groups. Pupils can often help each other at this stage. Ask pupils then to look at their orange words and to ask you *I think this means X in MT. Am I right?* You can then check their suggestions. Pupils then look at the words in red and ask the rest of the class first and then, finally, you can help them. The process of thinking about the meaning of the words allows time for pupils to understand rather than to learn them by rote.

- Pupils can write vocabulary puzzles for each other in pairs or groups.

- The **English Control Panel** will help pupils record words for revision.

- Pupils can practise vocabulary at home by making up their own exercises, as suggested in Units 1 and 2 of the Activity Book.

- Try to use as many of the new words in your own classroom language so that pupils hear them in other contexts and not just in the stories and texts in the book.

- Spend a few minutes at the beginning of each lesson asking pupils what they remember from the previous lesson.

Writing

What and why?

By now pupils will be expected to write in English in almost every lesson – some shorter pieces and some longer pieces. There are two main roles for writing in the language classroom. One sets the skill itself as the target – we would like the pupils to improve their writing skills such as spelling and punctuation in English. The second role views writing as a means of improving their English through practising new **vocabulary** and grammar.

Practical ideas

- Ask pupils to make notes in English before they work on an extended piece of writing, whether working alone or in groups.

- Ask pupils to keep a project journal in English when they do their **project work** in section D of each unit.

- When you are correcting written work, you could decide to take a different focus for each week:

Week 1 can be Spelling week, and you only correct spelling.

Week 2 can be Tenses week, and you only correct tenses.

Week 3 can be Punctuation week, and you only correct punctuation.

In this way, you and the pupils will be able to see clearly where they have specific problems in their writing, rather than having a page of corrections to decipher! Pupils will then be able to say, for example, *My spelling is pretty good, but I need more practice with my tenses.*

Games extra

Games are an active and enjoyable way for children to use new language and build up confidence. It is important that any games that you use really do involve using language and that the time you spend on the game has benefit for the children.

1 **Before starting a game,** it is important that all the children know exactly what they have to do. Explain in the mother tongue and get the children to explain back to you. The rest of the game should then be played in English.

2 **Encourage the children to use English** while they are playing. Giving them suggested language to use will be very helpful. You could write the language on cards to hand out or on a poster to stick up on the wall.

3 **A game is a good opportunity for you to use English naturally.** Example phrases:

Let's play a game.
Do you want to play a game?
Make a circle / two teams.
Sit on the floor.
Move your chairs over here.
Who would like to start / volunteer?
Who would like to be in the middle?
Who would like to be the team leader?
Find a partner.
Face your partner.
Play in / Get into groups of four.
Take it in turns.
Whose turn is it?
The winner is the person with the most points.
Sit down when you're out.
Ready, steady, go!

4 **Don't let a game go on too long.** It is best to stop while the pupils are still enjoying it – then they'll want to play it again. You can signal a natural end to a game by playing some music during the game. When the music ends, the game is over.

5 **Use games at different points in a lesson,** not only at the end – otherwise children can begin to see a game as a 'reward'. In many ways, a game can be just as serious and important as any other classroom activity.

6 **Keep everybody involved.** Games in which more and more children are 'out' (i.e. drop out of the game when they make a mistake) may be a lot of fun for the winner, but can be very demoralising for the others, as well as wasting their time. Aim to keep all the children in the game all the time, by using a point system, or by putting sticky labels on the children who would otherwise be 'out'.

The following are some suggestions for games that work well with children in classrooms where there is not a lot of space.

Present perfect sentences game

Write all the letters of the alphabet except *X* and *Y* on 24 separate pieces of paper. If you have more than 24 children, write the letters *B, D, E, L, M, N, P* twice. Divide the class into teams of four to six pupils. Give each child a letter, so each team has four to six letters. Give teams four minutes to write as many sentences as they can using the present perfect and their letters at the start of each sentence. For example, the team with letters *B, F, L,* and *S* could write:

Ben has been to Barcelona.
Frederico has climbed a mountain.
Lee has seen the London Eye.
Sara has had pasta in Italy.

Give one point for each correct sentence. The team with the most points wins.

The game can be played with different structures. For a revision focus, you could play it using different structures in each 'round'.

Present perfect miming game

Prepare sentences in the present perfect about situations that have just happened. These should be situations which the pupils can act out for the rest of the class to guess. You may prefer to work only with participles that the pupils have already seen in *Primary Colours 5* or to give them the opportunity to build on their knowledge through this activity. Here are some suggestions:

You have just eaten a very big dinner.
You have just seen a lion.
You have just run three kilometres.
You have just heard a funny joke.
You have just scored a winning goal in a football match.
You have just met an old friend.
You have just failed an exam.
You have just fallen off your bicycle.
You have just received a lovely present.
You have just been in a thunderstorm and are wet.
You have just dropped and broken your mother's favourite plate.
You have just woken up.

Pupils play in four teams. The teams take it in turns to send a team member out to the front. This pupil takes a sentence from the teacher and reads it. Check that the pupil understands the sentence.

He or she then mimes what has just happened for the rest of the team to guess. If they guess it within one minute, they get a point.

Variation

To encourage more use of language, you can allow the pupils who are miming to use some words and expressions, but they must not use any of the words in the sentence. For example, with the sentence about the lion, the pupil could say *Aaagh! It's going to eat me!* but they must not say *lion*.

Lexical sets game

This game is based on *Happy Families*.

Divide the class into groups of four. Give each pupil a piece of A4 card. They fold it into eight. Give these four lexical sets to the pupils:

1 Places in a town: *hotel, restaurant, supermarket, bank, newsagent*

2 Things on the carpet: *screen, control panel, button, control card, code*

3 Ways of using your voice: *scream, shout, whisper, reply, ask*

4 About Venice – *float, boat, wet, canal, gondola*

(Alternatively, pupils can choose their own 'sets'.)

They choose one set each and write one word on five of their eight squares. They then add three other words from their Pupil's Book.

They cut up their words and each group shuffles their 32 cards together.

One person deals five words to each pupil and leaves the rest face down on the desk with the top card face up. They take it in turns to take a word and to throw away one of their cards until the first person gets one set of five words and puts them on the desk for the others to check.

Time dominoes

Photocopy Cut-outs 3 and 4 on pages 129 and 130 for each pair of pupils. Ask the pupils to cut out the cards, reminding them that they should end up with two panels on each card as in the game *Dominoes*. They shuffle the dominoes and take fourteen each. The youngest player in each pair puts one domino in the centre of the table. The pupils then take it in turns to put a matching time next to one end of the chain of dominoes or the other, and to say the time. If a player cannot put down one of their dominoes, they knock on the table, say *What's the time?* and miss a turn.

If the pupils form a chain with the same time in numbers and words on either end, the next player starts a new chain. The first one to use up all their dominoes is the winner.

Future consequences

Give each pupil a piece of A4 paper. As you give each instruction below, remind the class to use the future simple with *will*.

1 At the top of the paper they write a name (male or female, for example someone in class, a celebrity, cartoon / TV character, etc.). They fold the paper over and pass it to the pupil on their right.

2 They then write what this person will wear in 20 years' time. They fold the paper over again and pass it to the pupil on the right.

3 They then write what the person will eat in 20 years' time. They fold the paper over again and pass it to the pupil on the right.

4 They then write where the person will live in 20 years' time. They fold the paper over again and pass it to the pupil on the right.

5 They then write what job the person will do in 20 years' time. They fold the paper over again and pass it to the pupil on the right.

6 They then draw and write how the person will travel to work in 20 years' time. They fold the paper over again and pass it to the pupil on the right.

At the end pupils open their papers and read out to the class what is on their sheet.

Design a board game

Ask pupils to design a board game with questions for the end of each unit of the Pupil's Book. The children could work in small groups to make and colour the game for others to play.

Story game

Pupils play in teams of four. In advance, photocopy the twelve story pages from Units 1–6 in the Pupil's Book. Cut off the words and then cut out the eight pictures for each unit and put them in an envelope. Give one envelope to each team. Pupils put the pictures in the correct order and write a sentence for each picture. The first team to complete the task with an appropriate sentence about each picture are the winners. The focus of this game should be on expressing the idea, not on accurately reproducing the story text from the Pupil's Book.

Unit 1 Extra practice

1 Complete the puzzle. Then number the clues.

James, Alice and Gary were in James'
parents' [5].
They found a ☐ there and Laya
appeared.
Gary ☐ the *Start* button.
☐ Laya appeared again.
She showed them a ☐ on the ☐.
The first place they went to was the ☐.
They saw some ☐ there.

```
1  A □ □ □ □ □ □ □ □ □ □
2 □ □ □ P □ □ □
     3 □ P □ □ □ □ □
4 □ □ □ E □ □ □
        5 A T T I C □ □ □ □ □ □
        6 □ R □ ▓ □ □ □ □
7 □ □ □ E □ □ □ □ □
  8 □ □ D □ □
```

2 Complete the sentences with 'must' or 'mustn't' and a verb.

1 If you travel in a car, you ....*must wear*.... a seat belt.

2 If you go to the cinema, you
....
a mobile phone.

3 If you ride your bike on the road, you
....
careful.

4 If you take food to the zoo, you
....
the animals.

5 If you have a picnic in the country, you
....
your rubbish home.

6 If you work in the library, you
....
a noise.

3 Match the parts of the sentences.

1 If you walk in the Grand Canyon in the daytime,

2 If you camp in the Grand Canyon at night,

3 If you see an adult female mountain lion,

4 If mountain lions are hungry,

5 If an adult male lion sees you,

6 If you see a young lion,

a ... they kill rabbits, sheep and deer.

b ... don't go near – its mother is always nearby!

c ... you can often see the tracks of mountain lions.

d ... it can be aggressive.

e ... you can sometimes hear the mountain lions hunting.

f ... she often has kittens with her.

4 Read the Grand Canyon Warden's animal watch diary. Complete his report.

Animal watch diary

Day	Animals
3	6 rattlesnakes (river)
7	3 mountain lions (forest)
10	12 sheep (path)
11	15 deer (rocks)
19	4 rabbits (forest)
21	2 elk (waterfall)

Animal Watch Report

On the third day I saw six rattlesnakes at the river.

5 Complete the sentences with 'too'.

1 ..The T-shirt was too expensive... so I didn't buy it.

book   film   mountain   ~~T-shirt~~

2 ....
....
so I didn't climb it.

3 ....
....
so I didn't read it.

4 ....
....
so I didn't watch it.

Unit 2 Extra practice

1 Write the past tense of the Group 1 verbs on the Great Wall and the past tense of the Group 2 verbs on the carpet.

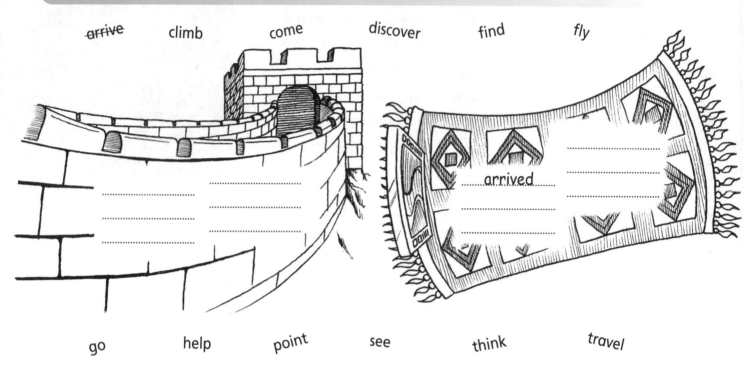

arrive   climb   come   discover   find   fly

arrived

go   help   point   see   think   travel

2 Complete the text with the past tense of the verbs.

appear   arrive   come   discover   fly   look   say   take   tell   think

People always ¹ ____thought____ that you could see the Great Wall
from space with your own eyes, but in 2004 a Chinese astronaut
² _____ that you can't. When he ³ _____ in space,
he ⁴ _____ around Earth for a day. He ⁵ _____
for the wall, but he couldn't see it. He ⁶ _____ back to
Earth and he ⁷ _____ everyone. The Chinese government
⁸ _____ that in future, books must give the correct
information. After this, American scientists ⁹ _____ amazing
photos of the Great Wall with powerful cameras and one of these
photos ¹⁰ _____ in Chinese newspapers, but it's true you
can't see the Great Wall from space with your own eyes.

3 What was happening at home while the children were travelling? Write sentences.

1 When the children were looking at the rattlesnakes, their friends were learning Maths.

2 ....

3 ....

4 ....

5 ....

6 ....

4 Modern China is changing very fast. Read the text. Then write the numbers in words.

China is the third biggest country in the world with a population of more than 1 billion ᵃ __one billion__ people. The country is very mountainous: 33% ᵇ .... per cent of the land is mountains and 10% ᶜ .... per cent of the land is hills. There are 53 million ᵈ .... pupils in secondary schools and 140 million ᵉ .... pupils in primary schools. Many of the pupils have mobile phones. Last year, about 440 million ᶠ .... people had a mobile phone in China. About 12 million ᵍ .... people, mostly students, have a computer. China has 132 million ʰ .... Internet users who use the Internet in Internet cafés. About 79% ⁱ .... per cent of the people who use the Internet are male students. 95% ʲ .... per cent of the people watch television. That's a lot of viewers!

Unit 3 Extra practice

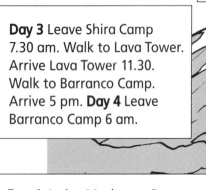

KENYA

Mount Kilimanjaro

TANZANIA

1 Look at the information. Complete the conversation.

Day 6 Arrive Summit 6 am.

Summit 5,895 m

Lava Tower 4,630 m

Barafu Camp 4,550 m

Day 5 Leave Karangu Valley Camp 6 am. Arrive Barafu Camp 11 am. Sleep all afternoon. Leave Barafu Camp 10.30 pm.

Day 3 Leave Shira Camp 7.30 am. Walk to Lava Tower. Arrive Lava Tower 11.30. Walk to Barranco Camp. Arrive 5 pm. **Day 4** Leave Barranco Camp 6 am.

Karangu Valley Camp 4,200 m

Day 4 Arrive Karangu Valley Camp 1 pm.

Barranco Camp 3,950 m

Shira Camp 3,840 m

Day 2 Leave Machame Camp 7 am. Walk 9 kilometres. Arrive Shira Camp 4 pm. Sign Visitors' Book.

Day 1 Arrive Machame Gate 11 am. Weigh luggage and give to guides to carry. Leave Machame Gate 2 pm. Walk to Machame Camp.

Machame Gate 1,490 m

Machame Camp 2,980 m

Day 1 Arrive Machame Camp 6 pm.

John: How many days will it take to climb Mount Kilimanjaro?

Guide: ¹ It will take six days. ....

Mary: That's a long time! So, what time will we leave on Day 1?

Guide: ² ....

John: Where will we sleep every night?

Guide: ³ ....

Mary: Will we carry our luggage?

Guide: ⁴ ....

John: How many metres will we climb to the summit?

Guide: ⁵ ....

Mary: When will we reach the summit?

Guide: ⁶ ....

John: Will we need anything special?

Guide: Lots of energy!

PHOTOCOPIABLE Unit 3 Extra practice

2 The Kilimanjaro guide tells John and Mary more about the trip.
Match the parts of the sentences.

1 If you forget anything,

2 If you have an accident,

3 If you walk slowly,

4 If you want to rest,

5 If you want special food,

6 If you are frightened,

a ... don't worry, we will look after you.

b ... we will spend another night in a camp.

c ... don't worry, we will give it to you.

d ... we will cook it for you.

e ... we will call for a helicopter ambulance.

f ... don't worry, we will wait for you.

3 Read about the hyrax. What do you think? Complete the table
with the numbers of the sentences.

[1] The hyrax is a small mammal which lives in Kenya. [2] It has two large teeth, like the tusks of elephants, in the top of its mouth. [3] The feet of the hyrax and the elephant look the same. [4] The blood of elephants and hyraxes is also the same type.

[5] Many years ago, hyraxes lived in Africa, Europe and Arabia. [6] Scientists say that some hyraxes were the same size as hippos.

[7] Hyraxes live in large groups with different mothers, fathers and their children. [8] When the young males are older, they leave their family group and make new groups. [9] Young male hyraxes can be very aggressive.

[10] When baby hyraxes are born, their eyes are open. [11] They have fur on their bodies and they can climb rocks immediately. [12] The hyrax has more bones in its back than any other animal. [13] They are good to keep as pets.

True sentences	False sentences
....	....
....	....

Unit 4 Extra practice

1a Find ten places in the puzzle.

H	E	P	E	R	M	I	C	A	F	E	P
F	U	S	C	H	O	O	L	C	A	S	O
B	R	E	S	T	A	U	R	A	N	T	S
B	K	E	N	E	W	S	A	G	E	N	T
A	H	U	H	L	G	Y	O	P	C	D	O
N	E	R	O	E	S	K	N	I	I	A	F
K	E	U	T	W	I	J	D	C	N	G	F
S	U	P	E	R	M	A	R	K	E	T	I
Q	U	D	L	K	R	E	V	U	M	H	C
Y	L	I	B	R	A	R	Y	L	A	M	E

1b Complete the sentences with six more places from Exercise 1a.

A ..library.. is a place where you can
.... read books and magazines ....

A .... is a place where you can ....

A .... is a place where you can ....

A .... is a place where you can ....

A .... is a place where you can ....

A .... is a place where you can ....

A .... is a place where you can ....

2 Write questions for the answers.

1
Have you ever been to the USA?

2
....
....

3
....
....

4
....
....

5
....
....

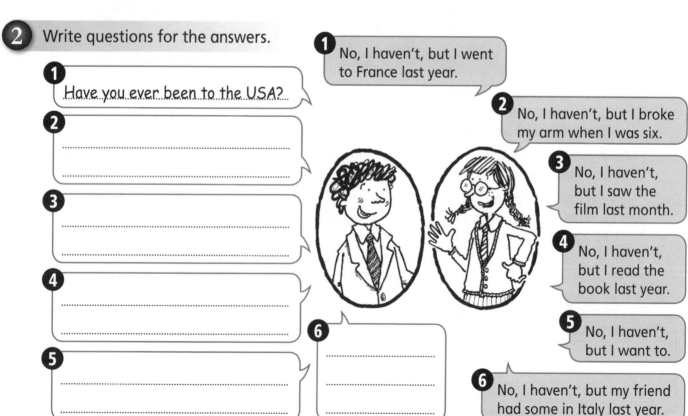

1 No, I haven't, but I went to France last year.

2 No, I haven't, but I broke my arm when I was six.

3 No, I haven't, but I saw the film last month.

4 No, I haven't, but I read the book last year.

5 No, I haven't, but I want to.

6 No, I haven't, but my friend had some in Italy last year.

6
....
....

3 Look at the map. Correct the sentences.

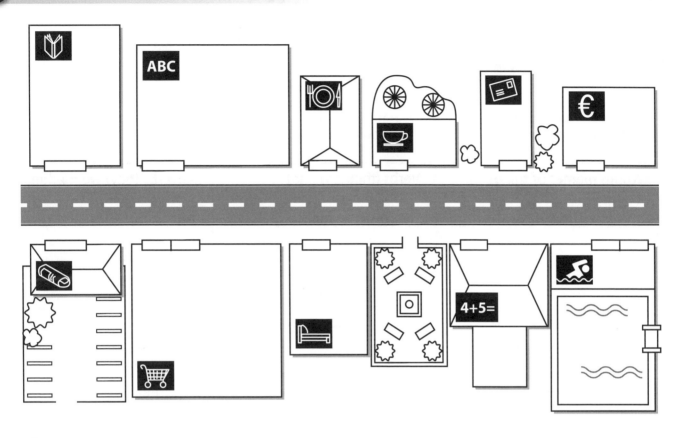

1 The square is opposite the school.
The square is opposite the café.

2 The library is on the left of the bank.

....

3 The supermarket is next to the café.

....

4 The café is on the left of the restaurant.

....

5 The restaurant is opposite the school.

....

6 The school is next to the post office.

....

7 The swimming pool is next to the cinema.

....

8 The newsagent is next to the hotel.

....

Unit 5 Extra practice

1a Write the words in the correct groups.

~~fall~~   put up   quickly   quietly   secret   slowly
snow   softly   tent   torch   turn on   whisper

Nouns (names of things)	Verbs (things we do)	Adverbs (how we do things)
....	fall	....
....	....	....
....	....	....
....	....	....

1b Write sentences about the pictures. Use a word from each group in Exercise 1a.

The children ....

....

....

....

....

....

....

....

2 Match the Rocky Ski Resort Rules with the reasons.

Rocky Ski Resort Rules

1 Always check that all your equipment is safe.

2 Always test new equipment before skiing on the mountains.

3 Don't ski immediately behind someone in front of you.

4 Don't stop in narrow places.

5 Always keep to the side of the path when climbing up the mountain.

6 Obey all signs.

7 Don't ski on a closed path.

a So you know how to use it.

b The doctors will not be able to find you if you have an accident.

c So that it doesn't break when you are skiing.

d They will help you ski safely!

e So people can ski past you easily.

f They can stop suddenly.

g People will ski down the middle of the path.

3 Write what has just happened.

They've just had pizza.

Unit 6 Extra practice

1 Label the picture.

body   cockpit   nose   ~~pilot~~   tail   wheels   wings

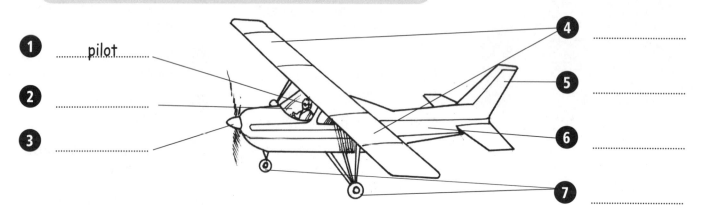

1 ....pilot..........

2 ....

3 ....

4 ....

5 ....

6 ....

7 ....

2 Complete the puzzle.

1 An electric piano can .... like a guitar.

2 What are you cooking? It .... like chicken.

3 This isn't cola! It .... like lemonade.

4 This painting is excellent. It .... like a photograph.

5 I don't know what this T-shirt is made of. It .... like cotton.

```
        1 S O U N D
      2   |       |   |   |
   3 |   | |       |
          4 |       |   |
   5 |   | |       |
```

3 Fred isn't happy on holiday. Write what he is thinking.

1 This coffee ......tastes...... like tea!

2 This bread .... like a piece of plastic!

3 This music .... like the CDs that my noisy neighbour plays!

4 This cereal .... like rabbit food!

5 This jam .... like fish!

106   © Cambridge University Press 2007   PHOTOCOPIABLE   Unit 6 Extra practice

4 Correct the sentences.

1 The children have just cleaned the attic.
The children have just arrived in the attic.

2 They have just started their journey around the world.

....

....

3 They have just been to the Great Wall of China.

....

....

4 Gary has just jumped off the carpet.

....

5 Alice has just pushed a button on the carpet control panel.

....

6 Gary has just started to change shape.

....

5 Complete the text with the correct past simple, past continuous or present perfect form.

Notting Hill in London ¹ __has__ just __celebrated__ (celebrate) this year's Carnival! It ² (be) ....
the 43rd year of the Notting Hill Carnival and everyone
³ .... just .... (say) that this
was the best ever! It ⁴ (start) ....
in 1964 when many people from the West Indies
⁵ (live) .... in London.
They ⁶ (want) .... to hear
the music of the steel drums. The steel drums
⁷ (come) .... from Trinidad
and Tobago. When the people ⁸ (live) .... in the West Indies, they
⁹ (make) .... the drums from oil drums or biscuit tins. Steel drum music is a
symbol of West Indian culture. Some years ago, the BBC ¹⁰ (play) .... steel
drum music for the first time for some important cricket games and now it's almost a tradition!

Answers

Unit 1

1

1			R	A	T	T	L	E	S	N	A	K	E	S
2	C	A	R	P	E	T								
3				P	R	E	S	S	E	D				
4	S	C	R	E	E	N								
5				A	T	T	I	C						
6			G	R	A	N	D		C	A	N	Y	O	N
7	I	M	M	E	D	I	A	T	E	L	Y			
8		C	O	D	E									

The clues should be numbered in this order:
5, 2, 3, 7, 8, 4, 6, 1

2 2 mustn't use
3 must be
4 mustn't feed / give it to
5 must take
6 mustn't make

3 2 = e 3 = f 4 = a 5 = d 6 = b

4 On the seventh day I saw three mountain lions in the forest.
On the tenth day I saw twelve sheep on the path.
On the eleventh day I saw fifteen deer on / at the rocks.
On the nineteenth day I saw four rabbits in the forest.
On the twenty-first day I saw two elk at the waterfall.

5 2 The mountain was too high so I didn't climb it.
3 The book was too boring / long / difficult so I didn't read it.
4 The film was too boring / late / long / serious so I didn't watch it.

Unit 2

1 Group 1 on the Great Wall: came found flew went saw thought
Group 2 on the carpet: climbed discovered helped pointed travelled

2 2 discovered 3 arrived 4 flew 5 looked
6 came 7 told 8 said 9 took 10 appeared

3 2 When James was throwing the stones, their friends were going home.
3 When the children were reading the code, their friends were doing their homework.
4 When Gary was controlling the carpet / they were flying to China, their friends were watching TV.
5 When Gary was pointing up the hill, their friend was cleaning her teeth.
6 When the boy was taking them to the cave, their friend was sleeping.

4 b thirty-three c ten d fifty-three million
e a / one hundred and forty million
f four hundred and forty million g twelve million
h a / one hundred and thirty-two million
i seventy-nine j ninety-five

Unit 3

1 2 We will leave at 2 pm (on Day 1).
3 We will sleep in (different) camps.
4 No, you won't carry your luggage. (The guides will carry it / your luggage.)
5 We will climb 5,895 metres to the summit.
6 We will reach the summit at 6 am on Day 6.

2 2 = e 3 = f 4 = b 5 = d 6 = a

3 All the sentences are true, except the last (13). Remind the class if necessary that modern hyraxes are not the same size as hippos now, but scientists think that, many years ago, they may have been.

Unit 4

1a

H	E	P	E	R	M	I	C	A	F	E	P
F	U	S	C	H	O	O	L	C	A	S	O
B	R	E	S	T	A	U	R	A	N	T	S
B	K	E	N	E	W	S	A	G	E	N	T
A	H	U	H	L	G	Y	O	P	C	D	O
N	E	R	O	E	S	K	N	I	I	A	F
K	E	U	T	W	I	J	D	C	N	G	F
S	U	P	E	R	M	A	R	K	E	T	I
Q	U	D	L	K	R	E	V	U	M	H	C
Y	L	I	B	R	A	R	Y	L	A	M	E

1b Possible answers (pupils write six sentences using these or their own ideas):
A café is a place where you can have a drink.
A post office is a place where you can buy stamps.
A school is a place where you can learn English.
A restaurant is a place where you can have dinner.
A newsagent is a place where you can buy a magazine / newspaper.
A bank is a place where you can get / change money.
A hotel is a place where you can sleep / spend the night.
A supermarket is a place where you can buy food.
A cinema is a place where you can see a film.

2 Suggested answers:
2 Have you ever broken your leg?
3 Have you ever read (name of book)?
4 Have you ever seen (name of film)?
5 Have you ever (pupils' choice of past participle + other language)?
6 Have you ever had pasta / pizza?

3 Possible answers:

2 The library is on the left of the cinema. /
The post office is on the left of the bank.

3 The supermarket is next to the newsagent / hotel. /
The restaurant / post office is next to the café.

4 The café is on the right of the restaurant. /
The cinema is on the left of the restaurant.

5 The restaurant is opposite the hotel. /
The post office is opposite the school.

6 The school is next to the square / swimming pool. /
The school is opposite the post office. /
The café / bank is next to the post office.

7 The swimming pool is next to the school. /
The library / restaurant is next to the cinema.

8 The newsagent is next to the supermarket. /
The supermarket / square is next to the hotel.

Unit 5

1a Nouns: secret   snow   tent   torch
Verbs: fall   put up   turn on   whisper
Adverbs: quickly   quietly   slowly   softly

1b Possible answers:

1 The children put up the tent slowly.

2 The girl whispered the secret quietly.

3 The boy turned on the torch quickly.

4 The snow was falling softly.

2 2 = a   3 = f   4 = e   5 = g   6 = d   7 = b

3 2 They've just bought a tent.

3 She's just woken up.

4 They've just climbed a mountain / arrived at the top.

5 The bear has just taken some biscuits.

6 They've just cooked a fish.

Unit 6

1 2 cockpit   3 nose   4 wings   5 tail   6 body   7 wheels

2

		¹S	O	U	N	D	
	²S	M	E	L	L	S	
³T	A	S	T	E	S		
		⁴L	O	O	K	S	
	⁵F	E	E	L	S		

3 2 feels   3 sounds   4 looks   5 smells

4 2 They have just finished their journey around the world.

3 They have just been to Brasilia.

4 James and Alice have just jumped off the carpet.

5 Gary has just pushed a button on the carpet control panel.

6 The carpet has just started to change shape.

5 2 was   3 has just said   4 started   5 were living   6 wanted
7 came   8 were living   9 made   10 played

Unit 1 Test

Name ....
Class ....

1 🔊 Listen and write the numbers (1–6). (5 marks)

 **a**

 **b**

 **c** [1]

 **d**

 **e**

 **f**

2 Complete the conversation. (5 marks)

| If they have babies   If you move   ~~If you see one~~   To be quiet |
| To stop them attacking   You mustn't go |

Tom: Are rattlesnakes very dangerous?

Lucy: Yes. ¹ ...If you see one..., you mustn't move. You must stay still and calm.

Tom: Why do you stay still?

Lucy: ² ...., so that it doesn't know that you are there.

Tom: Oh yes, because they feel vibrations when things move. But what happens if they feel you move?

Lucy: ³ ...., they can bite you, and that's very dangerous.

Tom: And what about monkeys? Are they dangerous?

Lucy: Sometimes. ⁴ ...., they can become aggressive.

Tom: So, what must you do if you see a monkey with babies?

Lucy: Stay away from them. ⁵ .... near them. But if you suddenly see them, you must stand still.

Tom: Why?

Lucy: ⁶ .... They can become afraid if you move suddenly.

 PHOTOCOPIABLE Unit 1 Test

3 Complete 1–6 with 'too' and a word from the box.
Then match the parts of the sentences.

(5 marks)

dark   difficult   ~~frightened~~   heavy   hot   slow

(1) Peter was .... too frightened .... to move   (a) so she didn't take them home.
(2) The bus was ....   (b) so we couldn't see anything.
(3) The Maths homework was ....   (c) so they arrived late for school.
(4) The cave was ....   (d) so he stood still.
(5) The coffee was ....   (e) so Lucy asked Emma to help her.
(6) The school library books were ....   (f) so Mr Hill couldn't drink it.

4 Write the correct words on the lines.

(5 marks)

a canyon   coral   ~~a fossil~~   a hole   layers   tracks

(1) This is a rock with an animal or plant from thousands of years ago. .... a fossil ....
(2) This is a place with very high rocks and a river at the bottom. ....
(3) This is under the sea. It's many different colours and it's beautiful. ....
(4) These are the marks that an animal makes when it walks. ....
(5) Rocks can have lots of these from different times in history. ....
(6) You can fall into this if it is deep. ....

5 Complete the text.

(5 marks)

~~amazing~~   below   calm   deep   frightened   over

My aunt and uncle went to the Grand Canyon a month ago. Their photos are
¹ .... amazing .... They walked on the glass bridge. The glass bridge is on top of the
rocks and you can walk out over the canyon. There is nothing ² .... your feet
– only the glass of the bridge! The canyon is very ³ .... and you can see the
river 1,220 metres under the glass bridge. My uncle stood on the bridge and looked down.
He saw the river but he was too ⁴ .... to walk so he didn't move. My aunt
told him to stay ⁵ .... and walk slowly. Finally, he got back to the rocks.
The next day they flew ⁶ .... the canyon in a helicopter. My uncle liked that.

Unit 2 Test

Name ....

Class ....

1 🔊 Listen and tick (✓) the boxes.

(5 marks)

1 How long was Hadrian's Wall in Britain?

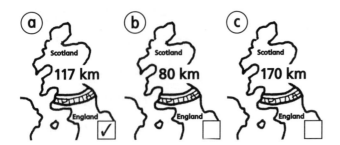

a Scotland 117 km England ✓
b Scotland 80 km England
c Scotland 170 km England

2 In what year did the Romans start building Hadrian's Wall?

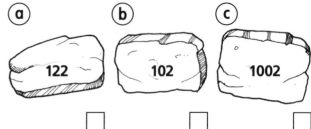

a 122 ☐
b 102 ☐
c 1002 ☐

3 How many soldiers built Hadrian's Wall?

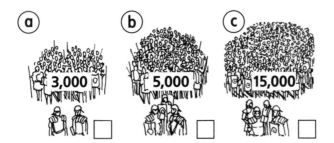

a 3,000 ☐
b 5,000 ☐
c 15,000 ☐

4 In what year did the Romans stop using the wall?

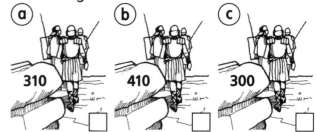

a 310 ☐
b 410 ☐
c 300 ☐

5 How many letters did archaeologists find at Hadrian's Wall?

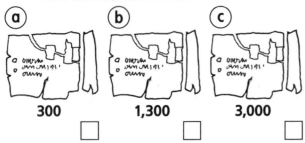

a 300 ☐
b 1,300 ☐
c 3,000 ☐

6 How many people visited Hadrian's Wall in 2006?

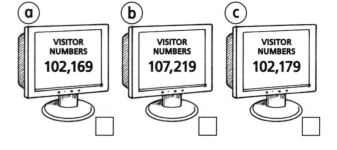

a VISITOR NUMBERS 102,169 ☐
b VISITOR NUMBERS 107,219 ☐
c VISITOR NUMBERS 102,179 ☐

2 Match the questions and the answers.

(5 marks)

1 How high is the Great Wall of China above the sea?

2 How deep is the Grand Canyon?

3 Is the Great Wall of China longer than Hadrian's Wall?

4 How wide is Hadrian's Wall?

5 Is the Great Wall of China very high?

6 Is Hadrian's Wall very old?

a Yes, it is 7.8 m tall in some places.

b It's between 3 m and 6 m across.

c Yes, the Romans built it about 1,900 years ago.

d The highest point is 980 m above it.

e Yes, Hadrian's Wall is shorter.

f It's 1,220 m from the bridge down to the river.

3 Complete the puzzle. (5 marks)

.... the river.

Turn .... by the big tree.

Go .... the trees.

Go to the .... of the hill.

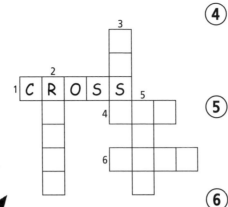
Climb .... the wall.

Turn .... by the rocks.

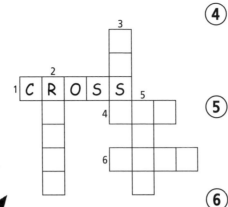

Crossword:

1 C R O S S

4 What was happening at six o'clock yesterday? Complete the sentences. (5 marks)

1 The sun ...... *was going* ...... down.

2 Robert .... on a wall.

3 His dog .... with a ball.

4 Sally and Ben .... home.

5 A donkey .... the river.

6 Some cows .... grass.

5 Choose the right words and write them on the lines. (5 marks)

My dad went to Hadrian's Wall about ten years ¹ ...ago... . He
arrived early ² .... the morning when it was dark.
There was a lot of mist and he ³ .... see the way.
He was lost. Then there ⁴ .... a noise. It was coming
towards him, so he hid ⁵ .... the wall. When the
mist went away, he ⁶ .... that it was a sheep.

1 past   before   ago
2 in   on   of
3 no   couldn't   can't
4 were   is   was
5 behind   in   under
6 seeing   saw   sees

Unit 3 Test

Name ....

Class ....

1 📻 Listen and write the numbers (1–6).   (5 marks)

a

b [1]

c

d

e

f

2 Look and read. Write 'yes' or 'no'.   (5 marks)

① The lion on the right is standing and eating. ......No......

② The lion on the left is watching the rhinos. ....

③ The giraffes can't reach the leaves on the trees because they are too high. ....

④ The rhinos are in the grass on the savannah. ....

⑤ The volcano is between the mountains and the jungle.

....

⑥ There aren't any plants on the mountains but there is some snow. ....

PHOTOCOPIABLE Unit 3 Test

3 Write the correct words on the lines. (5 marks)

> a guide book   a rope   ~~a sleeping bag~~   a stove   a tent   a torch

(1) This is warm to sleep in at night. ....a sleeping bag......

(2) You can use this to see in the dark. ....

(3) You can read this to learn about a place. ....

(4) You can cook food on this. ....

(5) You can use this to help you climb. ....

(6) You stay in this when you are camping. ....

4 Match the parts of the sentences. Then complete a–f with the correct form of the verb. (5 marks)

(1) I think we're going to Kenya in the summer

(2) If we go to Kenya,

(3) If we go to the savannah,

(4) If I see lots of animals,

(5) I won't go near the animals

(6) I think I'll feel hot in the savannah

(a) ... we (go) .... to the savannah.

(b) ... I (take) .... some photos to show my friends.

(c) ... because my mum and dad (read) ....were reading.... a guide book yesterday.

(d) ... because they can (attack) .... people.

(e) ... because it (be) .... usually very dry.

(f) ... we (see) .... lots of animals.

5 Read the story and write the missing words. (5 marks)

My aunt had a fantastic holiday in India last year but she had a problem with a monkey! She was walking up a mountain and she saw lots ¹ ...of... monkeys. She was hot and sat ² .... on a rock. She took her camera out of her bag. Immediately, a monkey appeared ³ .... it grabbed her camera. The monkey ran away at full speed. My aunt jumped up and fell off ⁴ .... rock. Suddenly, she was sliding down the mountain and it ⁵ .... very scary. Finally, she crashed into a small tree and stopped. If I ⁶ .... to India, I'll be very careful with monkeys!

Unit 4 Test

1 📻 Listen and tick (✓) the boxes.

(5 marks)

1 Where is the post office?

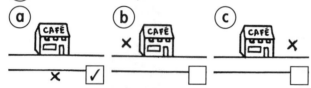

2 Where is the bank?

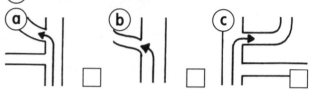

3 What shop does Emma need?

4 What time is the next water bus?

5 Where has Jim been?

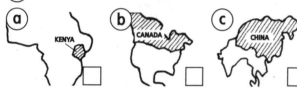

6 What hasn't Lucy done?

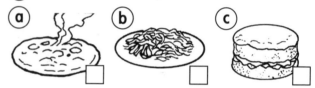

2 Complete the conversation.

(5 marks)

Come on.   ~~Have you ever been~~   Let's take a taxi.   We turn left   Where is it?   Yes, I can see

Sarah: I'm hungry. Let's go to the new da Vinci pizza restaurant.
David: ¹ ..... Have you ever been ..... there before?
Sarah: No, but I've heard a lot about it. I want to try it
            – everyone says the pizza tastes amazing.
David: OK. ² ....
Sarah: I think it's next to the canal, near the bridge.
David: Oh yes, I know. ³ .... ,
            go past the bridge and it's on the right.
Sarah: No, I think it's on the left, not the right.
David: You're right. ⁴ ....
            Let's go.
Sarah: If we walk, it'll take a long time.
David: Yes, and I'm very hungry. ⁵ ....
Sarah: What a good idea – you're a genius! And look, there's one here.
David: ⁶ .... that. Here, climb in!

3 Complete the puzzle. (5 marks)

1. You can have dinner here.
2. You can stay the night here.
3. You can buy magazines and newspapers here.
4. You can buy stamps here.
5. You can change money here.
6. You can have a drink here.

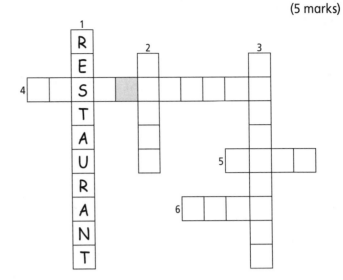

```
  1
  R
  E        2              3
4 S                       
  T
  A        
  U              5        
  R
  A        6              
  N
  T
```

4 Complete the text. (5 marks)

Josh	✓	✓	✗	✗
Beth	✗	✓	✓	✓

Josh ¹ ...has had... pizza but Beth ² ...hasn't... .
Beth ³ .... to the
mountains but Josh ⁴ ....
Josh ⁵ .... his
arm but Beth ⁶ .... Josh
and Beth ⁷ ....
in the countryside.

5 Read the text. Write one, two, three or four words to complete the sentences about the text. (5 marks)

My name is Sarah. Last year I went on holiday to Venice. One day I wanted to have dinner in the big square. I decided to take a water bus. The next one was at half past eight. I was late so I ran, but I fell and nearly broke my leg and my bag fell into a canal! Luckily, it didn't sink and a gondolier got it out with an oar. Finally, I arrived at the square but the restaurant wasn't open. I decided to go back to the hotel because my leg hurt and I was tired. I got back at ten o'clock and went to bed.

1. Sarah was ...on holiday... in Venice.
2. She wanted to travel to the .... by water bus.
3. She ran to the water bus ....
4. Her bag floated ....
5. She .... because the restaurant wasn't open.
6. She arrived at the hotel ....

PHOTOCOPIABLE Unit 4 Test

Unit 5 Test

Name ....

Class ....

1 🔊 What have they just done? Listen and draw lines. (5 marks)

Robert   Sally   William   Helen   Katy   Jane   Michael

2 Match the parts of the sentences. (5 marks)

1. If you are camping and there are animals near,

2. If you want to cook outside and there are animals near,

3. If you want to camp in a cold place,

4. If you want to walk in places where bears live,

5. If you see an animal with babies,

6. If you eat in the countryside,

a. ... don't move suddenly.

b. ... buy a warm sleeping bag and a good tent.

c. ... sing or talk in a loud voice.

d. ... don't leave your rubbish on the ground.

e. ... keep your food in plastic bags in a tree.

f. ... don't do it near your tent.

3 Complete the sentences. (5 marks)

left   put up   read aloud   switched on   turned off   ~~whispered~~

1. Jenny ..whispered.. quietly to Alex because she didn't want anyone to hear.
2. They arrived at the campsite and .... the tent.
3. It was dark so she .... the torch.
4. Anna .... from the newspaper to tell everyone the story.
5. She finished reading her book so she .... her torch.
6. Oh no! We .... food in our tent!

4 What have they just done? Write sentences. (5 marks)

Helen ......has just arrived.....
home................................. .

Harry ....
....

Tom and Sue ....
....

Emma ....
....

Ben ....
....

Peter and Lucy ....
....

5 Read the text and write the missing words. (5 marks)

I've ¹ ..just.. read about the Rocky Mountains. Lots of people live and ² .... in the mountains, for example there are farms and mines. Lots of people go there on holiday too ³ .... you can do lots of activities in the mountains, on the rivers and in the forests. You can camp in the Rocky Mountains, but if you camp, you ⁴ .... be very careful because there are bears there. ⁵ .... you see a bear, stand still and wait for it to move away. If you do that, you ⁶ .... be safe. One day I want to go to the Rocky Mountains.

PHOTOCOPIABLE   Unit 5 Test

Unit 6 Test

Name ....

Class ....

1 Listen and colour and draw and write.   (5 marks)

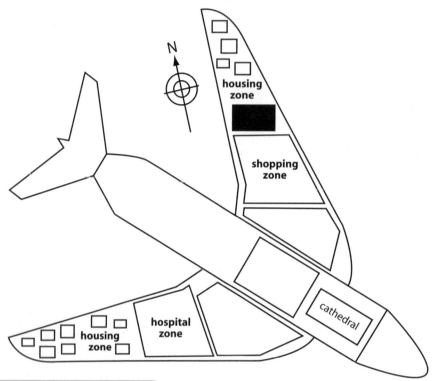

N

housing
zone

shopping
zone

cathedral

hospital
zone

housing
zone

2 Look and read. Write 'yes' or 'no'.   (5 marks)

NEWS

1. The men who are near the tower are whispering to the men who are working on the tower. ......No......

2. The tower where the men are working is black. ....

3. The girl who is crossing the bridge has just fallen off her bike. ....

4. The white tower is shorter than the black tower. ....

5. The boy who has just bought a magazine has dark hair. ....

6. If the boy who is reading the magazine doesn't look, he will walk into the girl with short hair. ....

3 Complete the puzzle. (5 marks)

Across

1 Computers are made of this.
3 The shape of Brasilia looks like this.
4 Birds and planes both have these.
5 The person who flies a plane sits here.

Down

2 You travel in this to fly to another planet.
3 This is a person who flies a plane.

¹M E T A L

4 Complete the sentences. (5 marks)

feels like   looks like   smells like   sounds like   tastes like

① Listen to that! It ....sounds like.... a plane.
② Can you see that cloud? It .... a bear.
③ Ergh! Touch this. It .... mud.
④ What's that noise? It .... the sea.
⑤ Mmm. This cake is nice. Try some. It .... banana cake.
⑥ I've never had this drink. It looks like coffee but it .... chocolate.

5 Read the text. Write one, two, three or four words to complete the sentences about the text. (5 marks)

My teacher went to Brazil in February. She flew there and visited Brasilia and Rio de Janeiro. They are very different cities. Rio is bigger than Brasilia and it is also older. My teacher visited buildings, museums and parks in Brasilia and she visited the beaches and mountains in Rio. One day she heard a noise and she thought it was drums. Suddenly lots of people arrived. They were playing music and dancing. It was carnival! My teacher doesn't like dancing but if you are in Rio for carnival, you must dance. So she danced all night!

① My teacher travelled to Brazil by ......plane...... .

② She visited two .... very different.

③ Rio is about four hundred years .... Brasilia.

④ The places where she visited in Rio were ....

⑤ The noise that she heard sounded ....

⑥ She doesn't like dancing but she danced .... carnival time.

Introduction

There are two main purposes for the tests. The first is to tell you how much the children have learned. The second is to tell you how effective your lessons are.

Contents of the tests

For every unit, there is a photocopiable test which should take about 30–40 minutes to complete. Each one contains five exercises based on the material presented in the Pupil's Book and begins with a listening activity. In all exercises, the first answer is completed as an example.

General approach

- Remember that formal testing is only one of a number of ways in which you can assess the class. See **A–Z: Assessment** on page 78.

- Give a test only when you feel that the class is thoroughly at home with the material in the unit.

- Present the test in a relaxed way, so that children see it as an extension of their normal class and homework activities, not as something 'special' or more weighty. Assure them that the test is meant to allow them to show how much they know, not to trip them up.

- Make it clear beforehand what is going to be covered in the test and give the children time to prepare.

- Introduce the lesson with a short warm-up activity to get the children relaxed and focused on English.

- Look at each exercise with the class before they start to answer and explain the task very clearly, using the mother tongue as well as the English instructions as needed. Then do the example with them before they set to work on their own. Encourage them to ask questions and go over the explanations again if necessary.

- If the children seem worried or uncertain about an exercise, go through one or two more of the questions orally before they begin to write.

Listening exercises

The listening material for the tests is recorded at the end of the appropriate unit on the cassette / CD and the tapescript is given, together with the answers, in the rest of this section. As with the other exercises, the first answer is completed as an example. Play the recording as far as the end of the example and make sure that the children understand what they have to do before continuing with the rest of it.

Play the whole recording at least twice and more times if necessary to allow the children to check their work.

Marking the tests

Each test carries a total of 25 marks. You can take in the tests to mark yourself or, as a more informal procedure, you might allow the children to exchange papers and mark each other's work.

Recording marks

You can use the photocopiable Assessment sheet on page 126 to record the children's marks in the *Extra practice* materials and these tests.

Interpreting marks

If all the children get over half the answers right, you will know that the class is going well. If a few children get less than half the answers correct, you may need to spend extra time helping those individuals and giving them encouragement. If most of the children get less than half the answers correct, you will need to think about why this has happened and what changes might be necessary in your teaching.

Alternative ways of using the tests

- You could choose to break the test into halves, giving you two shorter tests which can be completed quickly at the beginning or end of a lesson.

- If formal assessment through testing is not a priority, you might allow the children to work on the tests in pairs rather than completing them individually.

- If you don't want to test the children at all, you can use the test exercises as additional or alternative revision material in class or for homework at the end of a unit.

Tapescripts and answers

Unit 1

Tapescript (Exercise 1)

1 I want to look for birds in the Grand Canyon. There are lots of different types and I want to see as many as possible and listen to their singing.

2 I want to go on the water. You can go on a raft or a canoe on the river and the water moves very fast. It's very exciting!

3 I really like history so I want to look for fossils. The rock is very old and there are lots of fossils of sea animals in the rock.

4 I want to look for animals. There are lots of mammals and reptiles and some of them live very high up in the rocks.

5 I love rocks, but I don't want to look at them, I want to climb them. The canyon is very deep and it will be amazing to do that.

6 The canyon is very beautiful and there are lots of paths. I want to walk a lot and also to go on the glass bridge and look down at the river.

Answers

1 2 = e   3 = a   4 = f   5 = d   6 = b

2 2 To be quiet

   3 If you move

   4 If they have babies

   5 You mustn't go

   6 To stop them attacking

3 2 too slow = c   3 too difficult = e

   4 too dark = b   5 too hot = f   6 too heavy = a

4 2 a canyon   3 coral   4 tracks   5 layers   6 a hole

5 2 below   3 deep   4 frightened   5 calm   6 over

Unit 2

Tapescript (Exercise 1)

1 **Boy:** Mum, please can you help me with this quiz? How long was Hadrian's Wall? There are three possible answers here.

  Mum: Hmm. Let me see. No, eighty's too short. It goes across between England and Scotland. It's this one – 117 kilometres.

2 **Boy:** And in what year did they build it? Was it the year 1002?

  Mum: Oh no. That's too late. It was before then. Why don't you look on a website?

  Boy: Good idea! ... Right, it was in the year 122.

3 **Boy:** And how many soldiers built it?

  Mum: Ben, look at the website! It says three legions, that's a group of soldiers.

  Boy: But how many soldiers were there in each group? Ah ... I've got it. Five thousand. So three groups of five thousand is ... fifteen thousand.

4 **Boy:** And now in what year did they stop using the wall? Er ... it says about three hundred years later.

  Mum: Let's look at the three answers. OK, if they built it in the year 122 and they stopped using it three hundred years later, then the nearest answer is 410.

5 **Boy:** Number 5. How many letters ... how many **letters**?!

  Mum: Yes, a few years ago they found lots of letters at Hadrian's Wall. Let me see. 3,000? 1,300? No, not that many. 300, I think.

6 **Boy:** Last question! How many people visited it in 2006? OK, Mum. Here's a test. Was it 102,169?

  Mum: How do I know, Ben? Don't be silly!

  Boy: Or 102,179? Or, was it 107,219? Go on, Mum. Guess!

  Mum: 107 thousand ...

  Boy: No! It was 102,179. ... The answers are at the back of the magazine. I didn't realise before!

Answers

1 2 = a   3 = c   4 = b   5 = a   6 = c

2 2 = f   3 = e   4 = b   5 = a   6 = c

3

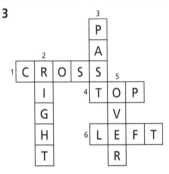

4 2 Robert was sitting on a wall.

   3 His dog was playing with a ball.

   4 Sally and Ben were running / were going home.

   5 A donkey was crossing the river.

   6 Some cows were eating grass.

5 2 in   3 couldn't   4 was   5 behind   6 saw

Unit 3

Tapescript (Exercise 1)

1 On my trip, I'll wear a warm coat because it will be cold. I'll go very high and I'll see the clouds. I'll see some birds and perhaps some small animal tracks.
2 On my trip, it will be dry and I'll feel hot in the day and very cold at night. I won't see a lot of plants or animals but I will see some camels.
3 On my trip, I'll feel hot. I'll see lots of big animals but I won't go very near them. I'll travel in a car to see them.
4 On my trip, it will be hot and wet. I'll see lots of trees and plants and I'll hear lots of animal and bird noises.
5 On my trip, I'll climb up high. I think it will be hot. If I feel vibrations in the ground, I'll be frightened! I'll probably see some small animals and some birds.
6 On my trip, I'll stay in a hotel. I'll take a guide book because I want to visit interesting places. I'll probably go to some museums and I'll have dinner in different restaurants.

Answers

1 2 = c 3 = f 4 = a 5 = d 6 = e
2 2 No 3 No 4 Yes 5 No 6 Yes
3 2 a torch 3 a guide book 4 a stove 5 a rope 6 a tent
4 2 = a will go / 'll go 3 = f will see / 'll see
   4 = b will take / 'll take 5 = d attack 6 = e is
5 2 down 3 and 4 the 5 was 6 go / travel

Unit 4

Tapescript (Exercise 1)

1 **Man 1:** Where's the post office?
  Woman 1: It's near here ... I think it's next to the café. Oh no, it's not – it's opposite the café.
2 **Woman 2:** Where's the bank?
  Man 2: Erm, go straight on and take the first, no, the second road on the right.
3 **Girl 1:** I want to buy a magazine. Can I buy one near here?
  Boy 1: Yes, you need to go to the newsagent. It's next to the post office and on the right of the supermarket.
4 **Woman 1:** What time is the next water bus?
  Man 1: Well, it's twenty past four now, so the next one is at quarter to five. Look, here it is, sixteen forty-five.
5 **Woman 2:** Jim, have you ever been to Kenya?
  Man 2: No, I've never been to Africa. I've been to Europe and also to Canada.
6 **Boy 2:** Lucy, have you ever cooked at home, you know, things like spaghetti?
  Girl 2: Well, I've cooked pizza and I've made a cake, but I've never cooked spaghetti. I don't like cooking with very hot water.

Answers

1 2 = c 3 = a 4 = b 5 = b 6 = b
2 2 Where is it?
  3 We turn left
  4 Come on.
  5 Let's take a taxi.
  6 Yes, I can see

3

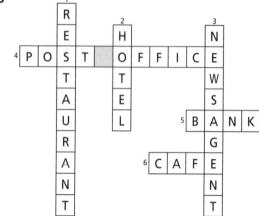

4 3 has been
  4 hasn't
  5 hasn't broken
  6 has
  7 have camped
5 2 (big) square / restaurant 3 because she was late
  4 in the canal / in the water / on the water
  5 didn't have dinner / didn't eat dinner / decided to go back
  6 at ten o'clock

Unit 5

Tapescript (Exercise 1)

William wanted to walk in the forest but he's frightened now. He's just seen some bear tracks.
Helen went for a long walk by the river and she's hungry now. She's just crossed the river and is walking towards the tent to get some food.
Robert is near the tent. He was also hungry so he cooked some food and he's just put it on his plate.
Jane is next to the river. She was looking at the plants and the stones under the water. She's just found a fossil and she's looking at it carefully.
Michael is standing in front of the tent. He's just woken up and is looking at William because William is frightened.
Sally went for a long walk with Helen. She's tired and has just opened the door of the tent because she wants to sleep.

Answers

1 Pupils draw lines to the children as follows:

Robert – the boy with the plate of food

Sally – the girl opening the tent

Helen – the girl walking towards the tent

Jane – the girl holding a fossil

Michael – the boy in front of the tent looking at William

2 2 = f 3 = b 4 = c 5 = a 6 = d

3 2 put up 3 switched on 4 read aloud 5 turned off 6 left

4 2 Harry has just woken up.

3 Tom and Sue have just played football.

4 Emma has just taken a photo.

5 Ben has just bought some biscuits.

6 Peter and Lucy have just had a pizza / pizza / some pizza.

5 2 work 3 because / and 4 must 5 If 6 will

Unit 6

Tapescript (Exercise 1)

1 **Man:** What can you remember about Brasilia? Can you find the housing zones in the wings?

Girl: Yes, I can see them.

Man: Colour the biggest superblock black.

Girl: The biggest one?

Man: Yes, in the North wing.

Girl: OK.

2 **Man:** Now can you draw something?

Girl: Yes. What am I going to draw?

Man: Find the bus station. It's next to the cathedral.

Girl: Oh yes. I can see it.

Man: Draw a bus in the bus station.

Girl: OK. Here's a bus.

3 **Man:** Do you want to colour now? Why don't you colour the cockpit?

Girl:: Where the pilot sits? OK. What colour?

Man: Colour it purple.

Girl: OK. I'm colouring it purple.

4 **Man:** And now for some writing. Can you see the hotel zones, in the wings but near the body?

Girl: Yes, I can see them.

Man: Write 'hotel' in the one in the South wing.

Girl: In the South wing?

Man: Yes, next to the hospital zone. Write 'hotel' in the square next to the hospital zone.

Girl: OK. I've written it now.

5 **Man:** Do you want to colour again?

Girl: Yes, OK.

Man: Colour the cathedral.

Girl: What colour? Oh, I know! The cathedral in Brasilia looks like a pineapple. Can I colour it yellow?

Man: Yes, that's a good idea. Colour the cathedral yellow.

6 **Man:** Last thing now. Can you colour the tail of the plane?

Girl: The tail?

Man: Yes, colour the tail green.

Girl: OK. Is that all?

Man: Yes, that's great. Well done.

Answers

1 Pupils colour, draw and write as follows:

Draw a bus in the square next to the cathedral.

Colour the cockpit purple.

Write 'hotel' in the square next to the hospital zone.

Colour the cathedral yellow.

Colour the tail of the plane green.

2 2 No 3 Yes 4 Yes 5 Yes 6 No

3

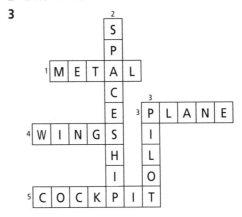

4 2 looks like 3 feels like 4 sounds like 5 tastes like
6 smells like

5 2 cities that are

3 older than

4 (the) beaches and (the) mountains / outside

5 like drums

6 because it was / at

Primary Colours 5 Assessment sheet

Class _____   Teacher _____

Child's name	Unit 1 Extra practice	Unit 2 Extra practice	Unit 3 Extra practice	Unit 4 Extra practice	Unit 5 Extra practice	Unit 6 Extra practice	Unit 1 Test	Unit 2 Test	Unit 3 Test	Unit 4 Test	Unit 5 Test	Unit 6 Test

Cut-out 1

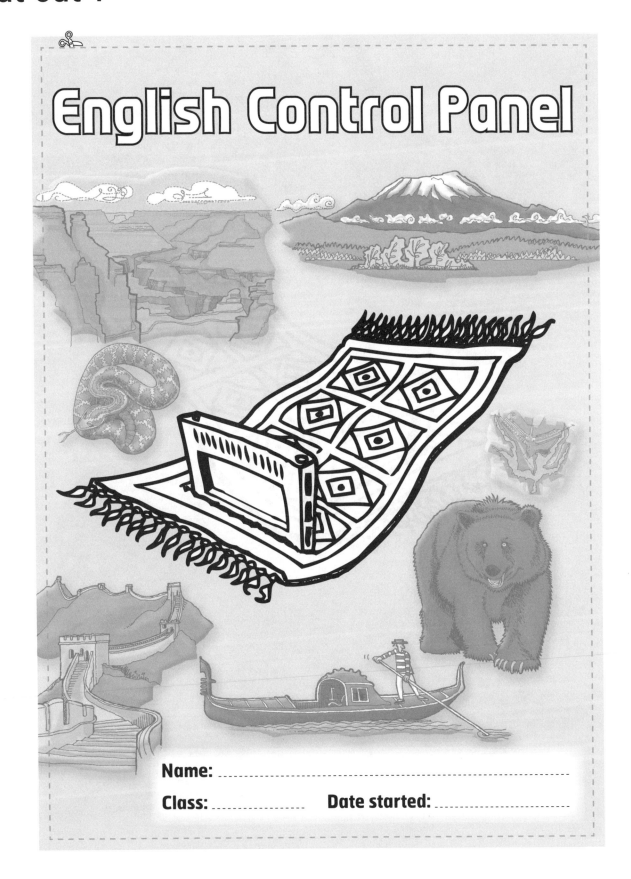

English Control Panel

Name: ....

Class: .... Date started: ....

Cut-out 2

Primary Colours 5
Cambridge University Press

PHOTOCOPIABLE Cut-out 2

Cut-out 3

13:10	quarter past five	16:25	half past three
18:45	half past twelve	14:10	ten past one
03:55	ten to eleven	21:10	twenty-five past one
15:30	five to four	05:15	quarter to seven
06:45	twenty-five to eight	05:45	twenty-five past four
23:25	ten past eleven	10:50	quarter to six
01:25	quarter to seven	23:50	ten past two

Cut-out 4

`07:35`	ten to twelve	`12:30`	ten past nine
`15:55`	twenty-five to eight	`11:10`	five to four
`18:10`	twenty-five past eleven	`19:35`	ten past six
`22:00`	twenty to ten	`19:30`	four o'clock
`21:05`	twenty-five to five	`20:20`	five past one
`04:35`	ten o'clock	`13:05`	half past seven
`09:40`	twenty past eight	`16:00`	five past nine

© Cambridge University Press 2007   PHOTOCOPIABLE   Cut-out 4

Word lists

Welcome!

attic
card
cardboard
carpet
cloth
code
fail
glass
heavy
light *adj*
made of
message
metal
paper
plastic
press
real
rectangular
round
rubber
serious
square
strange
wood

1 Laya's first clue

above
afraid
aggressive
ago
appear
away
beauty
below
button
canyon
climb
coral
decide
deep
deer
desert
exciting
expensive
far away
fossil

frightened
goat
grow
high
hole
huge
hurt
immediately
keep
layer
lizard
loud
map
old
ordinal numbers
push
raft
rattlesnake
screen
slow
somewhere
special
sting
stone
suddenly
throw
together
touch
tracks

2 A long way from home

add
beautiful
body
build (built)
cave
come (came)
control
cross
cry
dark
dead
distance
do (did)
donkey
emperor
enormous
find (found)
fly (flew)
go (went)
hard
hide (hid)
hill
left
light *n*
lost
marry
mist
numbers over 100
perhaps
point
put (put)
right
run (ran)
say (said)
see (saw)
shout
smile
soldier
statue
take (took)
tell (told)
temple
think (thought)
top
translate

3 On the mountain

bamboo
batteries
break
brilliant
chance
climate
clue
coat
countryside
eagle
fall (fell)
forest
grab
guide book
hit (hit)
hyena
hyrax
ice
idea
land
leopard
level
lobelia
mountain
rock
rope
savannah
scary
silence
sleeping bag
slide
snow
speed
stove
tale
tent
torch
wet

4 Water, water everywhere

amazing
be / go (been)
boot
bossy
break (broken)
bridge
canal
difficult
digital times
ever
everywhere
excellent
festival
few
float
go straight on
gondola
gondolier
have (had – pp)
historical
impossible
in front of
instead
it's on the (left)
make (made – pp)
mask
motorboat
never
next to
normal
oar
on the left / right
opposite
pick up
regatta
run (run – pp)
sand
sea
see (seen)
square *n*
take the (first) road on the (left)
timetable
turn left / right (at the ...)
unusual
write (written)

5 There's something outside ...

ability
across
aloud
back
biscuit
blind
buy (bought – pp)
campsite
can *n*
canoeing
cloud
eat (ate)
fall (fallen)
find (found – pp)
footprint
forward
gold
ground
hang
hear (heard)
just
landscape
leave (left)
mine
noise
outside
path
potato
put (put – pp)
put up
read (read – pp)
reply
rubbish
safe
shine
side
silver
sit (sat)
size
skiing
speak (spoke)
squirrel
still
sugar
take (taken)

turn off
vegetable
wake up (woke up, woken up)
whisper

6 Laya's final message
almost
blow
building
bus station
cathedral
change
cockpit
coffee
crown
face
feel
finally
get (got)
government
have (had)
hospital
hotel
in the middle
knock
know (knew)
last
look like
nearly
next
pilot
return
road
shape
sleep (slept)
smell
sound
stay *n*
string
taste
that (pron)
tie
towards
tower
where (pron)
who (pron)
windy
wing
zone

Flyers word list

See page vii for information about the Cambridge ESOL YLE Tests. The following words all appear for the first time at Flyers level. This list shows which words pupils meet in *Primary Colours 4* (PC 4) and *Primary Colours 5* (PC 5). It is likely that they will have met other words from this list in their previous years of English.

A

a.m.	PC 5
across	PC 4
actor	
after	PC 4
ago	PC 4
agree	
air	PC 4
airport	
already	
also	PC 4
ambulance	
anyone	PC 4
anything	PC 4
anywhere	PC 4
April	PC 4
arrive	PC 4
art	
artist	
astronaut	PC 4
August	PC 4
autumn	PC 4
away	PC 4

B

before	PC 4
begin	
believe	PC 4
belt	
Betty	PC 4
bicycle	PC 4
bin	PC 5
biscuit	PC 5
bookshop	
bored	PC 4
brave	
break	PC 4
bridge	PC 4
broken	PC 4
brush	PC 4
burn	PC 4
business	
businessman / woman	

bus stop	PC 4
butter	
butterfly	

C

camel	PC 4
camp	PC 4
card	PC 5
castle	
cave	PC 4
century	PC 4
cheap	PC 4
chemist('s)	
chocolate	PC 4
chopsticks	
Christmas	
circus	
club	
college	
comb	
competition	PC 5
conversation	PC 4
cook *n*	
cooker	PC 4
corner	PC 5
cut	PC 4

D

dangerous	PC 4
dark	PC 4
date	PC 4
David	PC 4
Dear ...	PC 5
December	PC 4
decide	PC 4
dentist	PC 4
desert	PC 5
diary	PC 4
dictionary	PC 4
dinosaur	PC 4
drum	PC 5
dry	PC 5
during	PC 5

E

each	PC 4
early	PC 5
east	PC 5
else	PC 4
Emma	PC 4
empty	
end	PC 4
engineer	PC 4
enough	PC 4
envelope	
environment	
ever	PC 5
everyone	PC 4
everything	PC 4
everywhere	PC 4
exam	
excellent	PC 4
excited	
expensive	PC 5
explain	PC 4
extinct	

F

factory	PC 4
fall	PC 4
fall over	PC 4
far	PC 4
fast	PC 4
February	PC 4
feel	PC 4
fetch	
a few	PC 4
find out	PC 4
finish	PC 4
fire	PC 4
fire engine	
fireman/woman (firefighter)	PC 4
fire station	
flag	PC 5
flour	

fog	
foggy	
follow	PC 4
footballer	PC 4
forget	PC 4
fork	
fridge	
friendly	PC 4
front *n*	PC 5
full	PC 5
fun	PC 4
fur	
future	PC 4

G

geography	
get off	PC 5
get on	
get to	
glass	PC 5
glove	
glue	
go out	PC 5
gold	PC 4
golf	
group	PC 4
grow	PC 4
guess	PC 4

H

half	PC 4
happen	PC 4
hard	PC 4
Harry	PC 4
hate	PC 4
hear	PC 4
heavy	PC 4
Helen	PC 4
high	PC 4
hill	PC 4
history	PC 4
horrible	
hotel	PC 5
hour	PC 5
husband	PC 5

I

ice	PC 4
if	PC 4
ill	PC 4
important	PC 4
insect	PC 4
interesting	PC 4
into	PC 4

J

jam	
January	
job	PC 4
journalist	
July	PC 4
June	PC 4
just	PC 4

K

Katy	PC 4
key	PC 4
kilometre	PC 4
kind	
knife	

L

language	PC 4
late	PC 4
later	PC 4
leave	PC 4
left	PC 4
let	
letter	PC 4
lie	PC 5
light *adj*	PC 4
light *n*	PC 4
little	PC 4
a little	PC 4
London	PC 4
look after	PC 5
look like	PC 4
lovely	
low	PC 5

M

made of	PC 4
magazine	PC 4
March	PC 4
married	PC 5
(marry *v*)	
maths	PC 4
May	PC 4
may	
meal	PC 4
mechanic	
medicine	
meet	PC 4
meeting	
metal	PC 4
Michael	PC 4
midday	
midnight	
might	
mind	PC 5
(Never mind)	
minute	PC 4
missing	PC 4
mix	PC 4
money	PC 4
month	PC 4
much	PC 4
museum	PC 4

N

news	PC 4
newspaper	PC 4
next	PC 4
noisy	PC 5
no-one	
north	PC 5
November	PC 4
nowhere	

O

o'clock	PC 4
October	
octopus	
of course	PC 4
office	
once	PC 4
other	PC 4
over	PC 4

P

p.m.	PC 4
painter	PC 4
paper	PC 4
past	PC 4
pepper	
perhaps	PC 4
photographer	
piece	PC 4
pilot	PC 4
pizza	PC 4
planet	PC 4
plastic	PC 5
plate	PC 5
player	
pocket	PC 4
policeman/woman	PC 4
(police officer)	
police station	
poor	
post	PC 4
postcard	PC 5
post office	PC 4
prefer	
problem	PC 4
programme	PC 4
pull	PC 4
push	PC 4
pyramid	PC 4

Q

quarter	PC 4
queen	

R

race	PC 4
ready	PC 4
remember	PC 4
restaurant	PC 5
rich	
Richard	PC 4
right	PC 4
ring	PC 4
Robert	PC 5
rocket	PC 4
rucksack	

S

salt	PC 5
same	PC 4
Sarah	PC 4
science	PC 4
scissors	
score	PC 5
secret	PC 4
secretary	
sell	PC 4
send	PC 4
September	PC 4
shelf	PC 4
(shelves)	
shorts	
should	PC 4
silver	PC 5
since	
singer	
single	
ski	PC 5
sky	PC 4
sledge	
smell	PC 4
snack	
snowball	
snowman	
so	PC 4
soap	
soft	PC 5
(softly)	

someone	PC 4
somewhere	PC 5
soon	PC 4
sound *n*	PC 4
sound *v*	PC 5
south	PC 4
space	PC 4
speak	PC 4
spend	
spoon	
spot	
spotted	
spring	PC 4
stamp	PC 4
station	PC 4
stay	PC 4
steal	
still	PC 4
storm	
straight on	PC 5
strange	PC 4
stripe	PC 5
striped	
student	PC 5
study	PC 4
subject	PC 4
suddenly	PC 4
sugar	
suitcase	
summer	PC 4
sure	PC 4
surname	
swan	
sweet(s)	PC 4
swing	

T

take	PC 4
tape recorder	
taste	PC 5
taxi	PC 5
teach	
team	PC 4
telephone	PC 4
tent	PC 4
thank	PC 4
	(Thank you)
theatre	
through	PC 4
tidy	PC 4
tights	
time	PC 4
together	PC 4
toilet	
tomorrow	PC 4
torch	PC 4
traffic	PC 4
turn	PC 4
turn off	PC 4
turn on	PC 4
twice	

U

umbrella	PC 4
unfriendly	
unhappy	
uniform	PC 4
university	PC 4
untidy	
until	PC 4
use	PC 4
usually	PC 4

V

visit	PC 4
volleyball	PC 5

W

waiter	PC 4
warm	PC 4
way	PC 4
west	PC 5
where *pron*	PC 5
whisper	PC 4
whistle	
wife	PC 4
will	PC 4
William	PC 4
win	PC 5
wing	PC 4
winter	PC 4
wish	
without	PC 4
wood	PC 4
wool	

Y

year	PC 4
yet	PC 5

Z

zero	PC 5

Acknowledgements

The authors and publisher are grateful to the following sources for permission to reproduce photographs:

Shutterstock: p. 97, GoGo Images Corporation / Alamy: p. 99, © David Boag / Alamy: p. 101, Shutterstock: p. 101, Shutterstock: p. 105, © Paul Gapper / Alamy: p. 107.

The authors and publisher are grateful to the following illustrators:

Lisa Smith, c/o Sylvie Poggio; Graham Kennedy; Ken Oliver, c/o The Art Agency; F&L Productions; Steve Elford, c/o Lemonade Illustrations; Kelly Waldek, c/o The Organisation.

Cover design, book design and page make-up by Pentacor**big**.

Cover illustration by David Shenton.

Tests written by Robert Partington.

Sound recordings by Anne Rosenfeld, RBA productions, at Studio AVP.

Freelance editorial work by Pippa Mayfield.

The publisher has used its best endeavours to ensure that URLs for external websites referred to in this book are correct and active at the time of going to press. However, the publisher has no responsibility for the websites and can make no guarantee that a site will remain live or that the content is or will remain appropriate.